# Big Tech and Democracy

# Other Books in the Current Controversies Series

**CONTROVERSIES**

# Big Tech and Democracy

## Lisa Idzikowski, Book Editor

**GREENHAVEN**
PUBLISHING

Published in 2022 by Greenhaven Publishing, LLC
353 3rd Avenue, Suite 255, New York, NY 10010

Copyright © 2022 by Greenhaven Publishing, LLC

First Edition

Articles in Greenhaven Publishing anthologies are often edited for length to meet page
requirements. In addition, original titles of these works are changed to clearly present
the main thesis and to explicitly indicate the author's opinion. Every effort is made to
ensure that Greenhaven Publishing accurately reflects the original intent of the authors.
Every effort has been made to trace the owners of the copyrighted material.

Cover image: mama_mia/Shutterstock.com

Library of Congress Cataloging-in-Publication Data

Names: Idzikowski, Lisa, editor.
Title: Big tech and democracy / Lisa Idzikowski, book editor.
Description: First edition. | New York : Greenhaven Publishing,
2022. | Series: Current controversies | Includes index.
Identifiers: ISBN 9781534508569 (library binding) | ISBN
9781534508552 (paperback) | ISBN 9781534508576 (ebook)
Subjects: LCSH: Technology--Social aspects.
Classification: LCC  T14.5 B548 2022 | DDC 303.48'3--dc23

Manufactured in the United States of America

Website: http://greenhavenpublishing.com

# Contents

## Chapter 1: Does Big Tech Pose a Threat to Democracy?

**Yes: Big Tech Poses a Threat**

**No: Big Tech Provided by Large Corporations Has Its Benefits**

## Chapter 2: Does Silicon Valley Unfairly Target Conservatives?

### Yes: Big Tech Does Target Conservatives Unfairly

# Chapter 3: Does Technology Feed Extremism or Other Harmful Behaviors?

*J. M. Berger*

There have always been extremist groups operating throughout the world. Extremism is not a recent phenomenon. The one difference today is that the internet makes it much easier for extremist networks to survive, spread their message, and recruit followers. This viewpoint specifically looks at two extremist groups: the Islamic State and White Nationalists.

## Yes: Technology Can Aid Extremism and Harmful Behaviors

*Megan Squire*

Extremists are making the most of internet sites to promote their beliefs and actions. When one of the big plastforms takes down extremist postings, it just pops up on smaller sites that are not as regulated, thereby making it almost impossible to remove extremist content from social media.

*McLean Hospital*

It's no surprise that social media may affect a person's mental health. Studies show that teens are particularly vulnerable to negative mental health outcomes because of the time spent on various social media sites. Therapists suggest limiting or even abandoning usage depending on the severity of a patient's mental health problems.

## No: Not All the Effects of Technology Are Extremist or Harmful Behavior

*Jillian C. York*

Just as the large CEOs of big tech companies can choose what to promote on their sites, people such as former President Trump can choose to spew lies and disinformation, according to this viewpoint. Users should turn away from tech sites whose content offends them.

## Chapter 4: Should Technology Be Changed for the Good of Society?

### Yes: Technology Should Be Changed for the Future Good of All

### No: Big Tech Has Many Redeeming Qualities

# Foreword

"Controversy" is a word that has an undeniably unpleasant connotation. It carries a definite negative charge. Controversy can spoil family gatherings, spread a chill around classroom and campus discussion, inflame public discourse, open raw civic wounds, and lead to the ouster of public officials. We often feel that controversy is almost akin to bad manners, a rude and shocking eruption of that which must not be spoken or thought of in polite, tightly guarded society. To avoid controversy, to quell controversy, is often seen as a public good, a victory for etiquette, perhaps even a moral or ethical imperative.

Yet the studious, deliberate avoidance of controversy is also a whitewashing, a denial, a death threat to democracy. It is a false sterilizing and sanitizing and superficial ordering of the messy, ragged, chaotic, at times ugly processes by which a healthy democracy identifies and confronts challenges, engages in passionate debate about appropriate approaches and solutions, and arrives at something like a consensus and a broadly accepted and supported way forward. Controversy is the megaphone, the speaker's corner, the public square through which the citizenry finds and uses its voice. Controversy is the life's blood of our democracy and absolutely essential to the vibrant health of our society.

Our present age is certainly no stranger to controversy. We are consumed by fierce debates about technology, privacy, political correctness, poverty, violence, crime and policing, guns, immigration, civil and human rights, terrorism, militarism, environmental protection, and gender and racial equality. Loudly competing voices are raised every day, shouting opposing opinions, putting forth competing agendas, and summoning starkly different visions of a utopian or dystopian future. Often these voices attempt to shout the others down; there is precious little listening and considering among the cacophonous din.

Yet listening and considering, too, are essential to the health of a democracy. If controversy is democracy's lusty lifeblood, respectful listening and careful thought are its higher faculties, its brain, its conscience.

Current Controversies does not shy away from or attempt to hush the loudly competing voices. It seeks to provide readers with as wide and representative as possible a range of articulate voices on any given controversy of the day, separates each one out to allow it to be heard clearly and fairly, and encourages careful listening to each of these well-crafted, thoughtfully expressed opinions, supplied by some of today's leading academics, thinkers, analysts, politicians, policy makers, economists, activists, change agents, and advocates. Only after listening to a wide range of opinions on an issue, evaluating the strengths and weaknesses of each argument, assessing how well the facts and available evidence mesh with the stated opinions and conclusions, and thoughtfully and critically examining one's own beliefs and conscience can the reader begin to arrive at his or her own conclusions and articulate his or her own stance on the spotlighted controversy.

This process is facilitated and supported in each Current Controversies volume by an introduction and chapter overviews that provide readers with the essential context they need to begin engaging with the spotlighted controversies, with the debates surrounding them, and with their own perhaps shifting or nascent opinions on them. Chapters are organized around several key questions that are answered with diverse opinions representing all points on the political spectrum. In its content, organization, and methodology, readers are encouraged to determine the authors' point of view and purpose, interrogate and analyze the various arguments and their rhetoric and structure, evaluate the arguments' strengths and weaknesses, test their claims against available facts and evidence, judge the validity of the reasoning, and bring into clearer, sharper focus the reader's own beliefs and conclusions and how they may differ from or align with those in the collection or those of classmates.

Research has shown that reading comprehension skills improve dramatically when students are provided with compelling, intriguing, and relevant "discussable" texts. The subject matter of these collections could not be more compelling, intriguing, or urgently relevant to today's students and the world they are poised to inherit. The anthologized articles also provide the basis for stimulating, lively, and passionate classroom debates. Students who are compelled to anticipate objections to their own argument and identify the flaws in those of an opponent read more carefully, think more critically, and steep themselves in relevant context, facts, and information more thoroughly. In short, using discussable text of the kind provided by every single volume in the Current Controversies series encourages close reading, facilitates reading comprehension, fosters research, strengthens critical thinking, and greatly enlivens and energizes classroom discussion and participation. The entire learning process is deepened, extended, and strengthened.

If we are to foster a knowledgeable, responsible, active, and engaged citizenry, we must provide readers with the intellectual, interpretive, and critical-thinking tools and experience necessary to make sense of the world around them and of the all-important debates and arguments that inform it. We must encourage them not to run away from or attempt to quell controversy but to embrace it in a responsible, conscientious, and thoughtful way, to sharpen and strengthen their own informed opinions by listening to and critically analyzing those of others. This series encourages respectful engagement with and analysis of current controversies and competing opinions and fosters a resulting increase in the strength and rigor of one's own opinions and stances. As such, it helps readers assume their rightful place in the public square and provides them with the skills necessary to uphold their awesome responsibility—guaranteeing the continued and future health of a vital, vibrant, and free democracy.

# Introduction

> *"Not long ago, information technology was heralded as a tool of democratic progress ... In recent years, however, doubts have surfaced about the effects of information technology on democracy."*
>
> —*Clara Hendrickson and William A. Galston*[1]

At first glance, big technology and democracy might appear to be unconnected concepts. Big tech is generally understood to be the biggest companies in technology with the most influence: Facebook, Google, Apple, Amazon, and Microsoft. Most people are reminded of scrolling on social media, looking up facts for school, meeting on Zoom, or ordering practically anything they might want or need when they come upon the term "big tech." When thinking about democracy they might remember a presidential election, or a history lesson from school about Thomas Jefferson or another founding father, or possibly recall news stories about the Black Lives Matter movement. Thinking about the two as a connected "big idea" affords an opportunity to look at each component in novel ways.

The public may or may not be surprised to find out that certain experts feel big tech poses a threat to society. A recent informal poll taken by Pew Research found that among technology experts, 49 percent felt that between 2020 and 2030 core aspects of democracy will be weakened because of digital technology. Interestingly, almost half of Americans, irrespective of political affiliation, feel that the US government should be stepping up efforts to regulate the technology industry more strongly.

Concerned individuals worry about a state of affairs dubbed "surveillance capitalism." As explained by Donell Holloway in the *Conversation,* surveillance capitalism is a process where personal data is for sale after it is collected through various means during surveillance of the internet. Often this is performed by the big tech companies without the knowledge or understanding of the hordes of people using search engines and social media platforms. Every like, dislike, computer search, purchase, or scroll on social media captures data which in turn is used in a new way for commercial gain. And the big tech companies are making tons of money by capturing, storing, and selling data. Ever notice how ads seemingly pop up out of nowhere after you've made an online purchase for a similar product? Data is continuously being collected and reshuffled to make more and more money. Can the big tech companies be blamed? After all that's what capitalism is all about—being successful and making money.

The stockpiling of data and the endless grab for money is not the only concerning aspect or effect of big tech on democracy. A frequent complaint from Republicans and conservative-leaning individuals and groups is that big tech is anti-conservative. Fervent believers of this anti-conservative targeting are former president Donald Trump, Republican boosters of the former president, and his supporters. Trump sees his permanent ban from Twitter as proof that the liberal tech companies are after him. Twitter explains the ban as a consequence of Trump's tweets, which they believe incited violence and insurrection. How many people understand that at the root of social media algorithms direct what users see on the various platforms, and their own engagement with content drives it all? It will be interesting to note whether Trump's ban is truly permanent.

Other unfortunate consequences of the digital world appear to grow out of human behavior. Lies, misinformation, cyberbullying, and the growth of cults, conspiracy theories, and extremism are increasing at an alarming rate. In a 2018 Pew Research poll, almost six in every ten American teens said they experienced abusive online behaviors, with name calling and spreading false rumors the most common type of abuse. Adults share the same type of negative digital consequences. In September of 2020, four in ten American adults reported being harassed, with 75 percent occurring on social media sites.

Amid all the doom and gloom let's not forget the good that individuals and society reap from technology via the big tech companies. During the COVID-19 pandemic digital access became a lifesaver. Many children spent school days learning online. People of all ages could see a doctor online through telemedicine. Hungry individuals ordered from a variety of food venues. Relatives connected when they could not physically be with loved ones. Online shopping made it safe and easy to get necessities. And streaming services made staying home a bit easier when people could watch their choice of entertainment.

With the controversy surrounding big tech, what if anything should be done with an eye towards the future? This part of the complicated whole is just as controversial depending on who is giving an opinion. Experts agree and disagree. Politicians agree and disagree. Everyday citizens agree and disagree. Governmental oversight is suggested by some. Some suggest letting the big tech companies themselves regulate the industry. Many people are angry or confused about the entire situation. One thing is certain: The debate over this complicated issue will and should not end.

The current debate surrounding this interesting topic can be investigated and understood by reading and contemplating the diverse viewpoints within *Current Controversies: Big Tech and Democracy,* which sheds light on this ongoing contemporary issue.

*Endnotes*

1. "Big Tech Threats: Making Sense of the Backlash Against Online Platforms," Clara Hendrickson and William A. Galston, Brookings, May 28, 2019. https://www.brookings.edu/research/big-tech-threats-making-sense-of-the-backlash-against-online-platforms/.

# CHAPTER 1

# Does Big Tech Pose a Threat to Democracy?

# Overview: What Are Big Tech's Capabilities?

*John Harris*

*John Harris is a columnist for the* Guardian, *writing about music, popular culture, and politics.*

Zoom being Zoom, Tim Berners-Lee's name appears in my browser window about 20 seconds before his audio and video feed kick in—and for a brief moment, the prospect of talking online to the inventor of the world wide web seems so full of symbolism and significance that it threatens to take my breath away.

During the hour we spend talking, that thought never fully recedes—but the reality is inevitably rather more prosaic: a 65-year-old man in a slightly crumpled, light blue polo shirt, talking—usually at high speed—from his home a dozen or so miles from Oxford, at a desk positioned just next to a fancy-looking model house ("I think that's a mansard roof," he says). For all that he is one of a tiny group of people who can claim to have fundamentally changed how most of us live—which explains why he had a role in Danny Boyle's opening ceremony for the 2012 Olympics—he carries himself with a striking lack of star power. He could probably walk down the average high street unrecognised; as if to underline that the human race may now have its priorities slightly wrong, at 345,000, his Twitter followers number less than 5% of Piers Morgan's.

Just over 30 years have passed since Berners-Lee, who was then working at the Swiss HQ of Cern (AKA the European Organisation for Nuclear Research, and the largest particle physics laboratory in the world) came up with the initial idea for the world wide web, conceived at first as a way of easily sharing research documents. (While the terms are now used synonymously, the

"Tim Berners-Lee: 'We Need Social Networks Where Bad Things Happen,'" by John Harris, Guardian News and Media Limited, March 15, 2021. Reprinted by permission.

internet is the physical network of interconnected computers and dates back to the 60s, while the web of Berners-Lee's invention is the system that enables information to be exchanged using the internet's connections.)

His idea was labelled "vague but exciting" by one of his bosses, but once he had built the first browser and website, interest and involvement in it soon snowballed. There was, however, one fascinating and inevitable twist: unlike the kind of inventors who patent their creations and keep some measure of control over what happens to them, Berners-Lee introduced his work to the world, and then simply watched what millions of people did with it.

That said, via the World Wide Web Foundation, founded in 2008 to "advance the open web as a public good and a basic right," he has long been a key voice in the global conversation about the online world and where it is taking us. Since 2017, the foundation has published an annual letter by Berners-Lee on 12 March, the web's anniversary. This year's deals with a huge issue highlighted and intensified by the pandemic: the fact that 2.2 billion young people across the world are lacking the stable internet access they need to learn online. From there, it pays tribute to a handful of young trailblazers who have recently used the web for such projects as turning plastic waste into personal protective equipment and working to protect "women, non-binary people and other at-risk individuals" in some south Asian countries. And it makes the case for technology that is "helpful, not harmful; inclusive, not exclusive."

The latter point comes down to online abuse, bullying and harassment, and the way that these aspects of online life disproportionately affect young people. Among Berners-Lee's arguments is the insistence things could easily be safer and more humane, if the people who build big platforms thought more carefully about their users. Blocking functions and other such tools, allowing people to focus their engagement on trusted friends, are hardly complicated, he says, but they often seem to be. "You need all those controls to be simple and obvious enough to be used by young people. That's one example. Another thing is, if you're asking people if they've experienced any problems, you have to speak to them in their language. People don't think, 'That was online abuse.' They think, 'That hurt.' You need to talk to them in their language, and make it clear that they have options."

The letter pointedly refers to "the toxic internet." Can he explain what that means to him?

"Well, you're not a feminist blogger," he says. "If you were, you wouldn't ask me that. If you're a woman, you can have a fine time until the one moment you get picked on. And it can be psychologically very, very extreme. The toxic internet is something that young people have less ability to manage. Women will be more susceptible. LGBTQ people, typically, are much more likely to be picked as a target. The toxic internet isn't something I experience at all. You may not."

By way of pointing towards something better, he talks about the possibility of "social networks where bad things happen less". He mentions Twitter's Birdwatch project, which encourages its users to flag up misinformation, and also mentions his idea of social media platforms offering their users "stretch-friends"—people from way beyond their usual circles, who might enhance their understanding of the wider world. "Suppose we build community curation systems, just like Wikipedia is a community curation system for an encyclopedia," he says. "Can we build real-time curation systems for what we think is appropriate? Can we build systems that lead people to being more constructive, and more likely to understand what it's like to be on the other side of a cultural divide, and more likely to figure out what these other people who speak different languages are like?"

It might seem as if nastiness, loathing and what the US academic Shoshana Zuboff calls "surveillance capitalism" are wired into the modern web as a matter of design, but Berners-Lee argues that reshaping the online realm along more positive, human-centred lines might be simpler than it seems. To illustrate his point, he talks about the widely acclaimed Netflix docudrama *The Social*

*Dilemma*, which traces the dire effects on a family—in particular, a young brother and sister—of an addictive internet strewn with lies and conspiracy theories, and platforms seemingly configured to maximise the profile of those things.

"It makes the case against one particular way in which things go wrong," he says. "It talks about a family who use social media, and they use advertising, and they are manipulated by the AI in the social network to maximise engagement, which maximises engagement with nasty stuff. So they end up believing a bunch of conspiracy theories, and the family becomes a very broken subset of humanity, just as a result of interacting with the social network. It's powerful.

"But then you should step back. It's making a good case about how one particular wave of social networks can work, if you train the AI to maximise the engagement of the teenager. But if you train the AI to maximise the happiness of the teenager, or the efficiency of the teenager—well, then the whole thing would produce a very different outcome. You use the same software—you just turn the dial. You could imagine two social networks where most of the code is mostly the same—it's just that one is optimised for one thing, and the other is optimised for another. And the unintended consequences in each case are completely different."

Berners-Lee's backstory goes back to the first stirrings of the tech age. His parents, Conway Berners-Lee and Mary Lee Woods, were part of the team that produced the Ferranti Mark 1, the world's first commercially available digital computer. He was a childhood trainspotter and, after graduating from Oxford (in physics), his working life began with a job at the now defunct British electronics firm Plessey (whose recruitment ads sometimes featured the enticing slogan "good job, good company"). After a first stint at Cern that ended in 1980, he spent three years at Image Computer Systems, based in Bournemouth. If all of this sounds almost comically mundane, there are things in his cuttings file that perhaps betray a romantic, future-gazing kind of mindset: when his two children were growing up, he would apparently make a habit of telling them that: "Everything you don't understand is magic."

He is now a professorial fellow of computer science at Oxford University, but focuses most of his working life on Massachusetts Institute of Technology (MIT) in Boston, where he has been working for four years on a fascinating project called Solid (more of which in a moment). Like most of the internet's pioneers, he began his journey through the past three decades with hopes that verged on the utopian and endured for a long time. In 2010, he may have warned against big social networks threatening the web's "single, universal information space," but in 2014, he was still enthusiastically making the case for how its global connections could "transform presidential elections, overturn authoritarian regimes ... and enrich our social networks." He says it was not until the watershed year of 2016 that he fully realised how drastically things had changed.

For the first phase of the web's progress, he had a set of stock lines about how people's use of it would tend to keep everything on the moral straight and narrow. "People complained about junk being on there," he says, cracking a smile at the quaintness of the memory. "They said, 'Well, you made this thing, and I found some nonsense on it.' And for many years, I would say, 'The web is a neutral platform. Humanity uses it, and humanity is good and bad, across the spectrum. What you have to do is just to nurture your bookmark list: take off the things that haven't served you well, and nurture all the things that have served you well, and blog about them, and link to them.'"

For a while, he says, he thought this worked. "People read each other's blogs, and they linked to blogs they thought were brilliant, and the blogosphere became this incredibly rich medium. In those days, I and all the people I knew curated a web of good stuff. And there was good stuff: there were blogs, and then Wikipedia came along, and there were search engines that found stuff out really quickly."

By 2016, he says, "people were still curating their bookmarks"—or, rather, consuming and propagating material they found on Facebook and Twitter—and among his liberal-inclined friends and associates, he says this seemed to be as positive and truth-promoting as ever.

"Meanwhile, there were far-right people, who were also quite happy with the web, bookmarking articles pointing to complete garbage, and conspiracy theories, and things that were completely untrue. So I realised that I and the people I knew were in a huge bubble. In the States, they were in a blue bubble, and then there was a red bubble … but it was no skin off our nose that there was this other red bubble. Apart from one thing: the people in the other bubble had the vote. And they believed all kinds of nonsense things, like the idea that they would get £350m a week [for the NHS] if we pulled the Brexit plug. After Brexit and Trump, I think a lot of people realised: 'We need to have a web that spreads more truth than rubbish.' And at that point, the Web Foundation said: 'It's not just about getting the web to everyone, it has to serve humanity in a positive way.'"

This basic argument has now belatedly started to make its way into politics, something seen in both an increasingly loud conversation about the responsibilities of the big platforms for misinformation and hate speech—and the accompanying conversation about tackling the same platforms' huge concentrations of power. On this stuff, Berners-Lee's opinions are delicately balanced. To take two topical examples, he is opposed to Australia's plans to force tech giants to pay news organisations even for the use of links to their articles ("the right to link is really important—it's just part of free speech, and it makes the web functional"), though when I ask him about the possibility of Google and Facebook being forcibly broken up, he sounds at least open to the idea.

Dominance of the web by a tiny handful of companies, he reminds me, is hardly new, but over the years, things have always shifted. Look at the history of browsers: Netscape was succeeded by Internet Explorer, which in turn was nudged aside by Google Chrome and Apple's Safari.

To that, there is an obvious riposte. The position of the 21st century's big players looks very different.

"I think what the American public and lawmakers are doing … I think they're aware of that," he replies. "And they know from experience with big oil and with [the American telecoms utility] AT&T, that there have been times when US governments have broken up large companies. There's a lot of discussion of that right now, and so that is a possibility."

Is it a possibility he supports? Would he like Google and Facebook to be broken up?

"I think it's more complicated than that. I think it's reasonable for the Federal Trade Commission to be strengthened, and be empowered to look at it, and to do the analysis. What you could do with these sorts of things is …" A very long pause, then he resumes. "You also need to talk to legal experts. But the US government does have the tools necessary."

Since 2016, Berners-Lee and some of his colleagues at MIT have been working on another way of challenging big tech's power: starting to reconfigure the web so that its users own and control their data, which might in turn power a more diverse and decentralised internet. This is the basis of the Solid project, which now has spawned a new startup called Inrupt. It all works on the basis of users controlling their data in online storage spaces called Personal Online Data Stores, or Pods. ("That's in the cloud—or, if you're really geeky, you have it at home, sitting in a physical box.") An increasing range of newly built apps are being designed to work with this new model: instead of surrendering their data to be indiscriminately used by big platforms, Solid users will judiciously allow everything from social media sites to shopping services to access their personal information on a case-by-case basis.

Even if he is uncomfortable with the phrase surveillance capitalism ("The world is more complicated than just sticking a term on things," he says), what he is working on will undermine that business model, if it is successful, won't it? "Yeah. It turns the world the right way round. The idea of surveillance capitalism depends on your data going, by default, to somebody else, and Solid's default is that it goes to you."

Though Inrupt is now working on the Solid "privacy platform" with such organisations as the BBC, the NHS and NatWest bank, its first stirrings seem terribly quiet: the day before we talk, I sign up to an embryonic, Solid-based social media platform called Ibex, but 36 hours later, my one post ("Hello all—Monday in the UK, and everything is coming apart … Is anyone there?") remains unanswered. This, says Berners-Lee, is because more work has so far gone into the project's technological nuts and bolts than its apps. I want to apply all the Steve Jobs criteria—it should be simple, and it should be sweet: 'I want one of those.'"

Does he have a time frame for that?

"I think it'll probably take a year or two. But if you're a developer, then this is the time to join in."

Not for the first time, despite his worries and misgivings about where his invention has ended up, he sounds convincingly optimistic. And, I wonder: amid the voices telling us that the web has turned out to be a dystopian hell, does that feel like a lonely vocation?

"No. My day job is at Inrupt, working on Solid. We're very, very positive. We're building systems which are demonstrably fairer, demonstrably more constructive, which demonstrably give power to the user."

Just for a moment, he slows down. "I'm lucky. It's a very positive environment to be in. The people I'm working with have bright lights in their eyes."

# Surveillance Capitalism Is a Threat

*Joanna Kavenna*

*Joanna Kavenna is a writer based in England. Her work has appeared in a variety of venues and includes novels, essays, and travel writing.*

It's a beautiful day on Hampstead Heath, the last weekend of summer—parliament is still prorogued. In a festival tent at the HowtheLightGetsIn festival, Professor Shoshana Zuboff is talking about her recent book, *The Age of Surveillance Capitalism: The Fight for a Human Future at the New Frontier of Power*. Zuboff stands on a low stage, making eye-contact with her audience. She spies someone who seems unconvinced, invites them to raise their concerns. "When this book was published in January, I left home for three weeks on the road," she says. "I'm still going."

The audience laughs. Because *The Age of Surveillance Capitalism*—a 700-plus page sociological analysis of the digital era—has become an epoch-defining international bestseller, drawing comparisons to revolutionary works such as Rachel Carson's *Silent Spring*. Naomi Klein has urged everyone to read it "as an act of digital self-defence".

It describes how global tech companies such as Google and Facebook persuaded us to give up our privacy for the sake of convenience; how personal information ("data") gathered by these companies has been used by others not only to predict our behaviour but also to influence and modify it; and how this has had disastrous consequences for democracy and freedom. This is the "surveillance capitalism" of the title, which Zuboff defines as a "new economic order" and "an expropriation of critical human rights that is best understood as a coup from above".

Later, in an unglamorous spot by some parked vans, Zuboff explains why she wrote her book. She has dark eyes behind horn-rimmed glasses; abundant black curls; a low, resonant voice. She is

"Shoshana Zuboff: 'Surveillance Capitalism Is an Assault on Human Autonomy'," by Joanna Kavenna, Guardian News and Media Limited, October 4, 2019. Reprinted by permission.

brilliantly erudite and outlines her argument in trenchant, honed phrases, as if reading aloud. Her work on the themes of *The Age of Surveillance Capitalism* began as far back as the late 1970s. She was a postgraduate at Harvard, writing a doctorate on the Industrial Revolution. To earn money, she became an organisational change consultant, working in offices that were "computerising" for the first time. "They were expecting immediate productivity, growth, efficiency. But it was chaos, disaster. Crazy stuff was happening. People were saying 'My work is floating in space!'"

In 1978, Zuboff was working at the *Washington Post*, with linotypists who were converting to cold type. "One day I had just finished the graveyard shift, and I wandered into the National Gallery of Art, where I saw these hulking, dirty, dark entities in the pit of a bright white amphitheatre." It was the Voltri-Bolton series by David Smith—an American sculptor who in the 1960s created sculptures from old factory machinery and debris. "I realised then the process of computerisation would be the next industrial revolution, and it would change everything—including how we think, and feel and how we create meaning. I had a notebook, and I started writing. This has been the agenda for my intellectual life since then."

This led to Zuboff's first book *In the Age of the Smart Machine: The Future of Work and Power* (1988)—a startlingly prophetic analysis of how information technology would transform working lives. Long before the emergence of the internet, Zuboff argued that everything that could be translated into information would be—exchanges, events, objects—and that data streams would be used wherever possible for surveillance and control. It was followed by *The Support Economy: Why Corporations Are Failing Individuals and the Next Episode of Capitalism* (2002), co-authored with her husband, James Maxmin, a former CEO of companies including Laura Ashley and a Distinguished Scholar at MIT, who died in 2016.

On the strength of her first book, Zuboff became one of the first tenured women at Harvard Business School. She later became one of the youngest professors to receive an endowed chair. With her husband, Zuboff went to live in rural Maine; they raised their children, farmed deer. In 2009, their home was struck by lightning and burned to the ground. The family escaped, but lost all their possessions - books, research materials, passports. "One odd thing: when the house burned, that old notebook from DC survived." Not long after this, Zuboff began to write *Surveillance Capitalism*.

It is the story of the digital revolution, and how the early utopian prospects of the web darkened into "a rogue mutation of capitalism marked by concentrations of wealth, knowledge and power unprecedented in human history." Gmail was launched in 2004; Google subsequently admitted that it has scanned private correspondence for personal information. In the same year, Facebook was founded, its business model also based on the capture of and access to personal information. The metaphor Zuboff uses is one of conquest: "With so little left that could be commodified, the last virgin territory was private human experience." In 1986, 1% of the world's information was digitised. In 2013, it was 98%.

It is a movement founded on predictive algorithms, mathematical calculations of human behaviour. Surveillance capitalists "sell certainty to business customers who would like to know with certainty what we do. Targeted adverts, yes, but also businesses want to know whether to sell us a mortgage, insurance, what to charge us, do we drive safely? They want to know the maximum they can extract from us in an exchange. They want to know how we will behave in order to know how to best intervene in our behaviour." The best way to make your predictions desirable to customers is to ensure they come true: "to tune and herd and shape and push us in the direction that creates the highest probability of their business success". There's no way "to dress this up as anything but behavioural modification". In 2012 and 2013, Facebook conducted "massive-scale contagion experiments" to see if they could "affect real-world emotions and behaviour, in ways that bypassed user awareness."

There are crux points in the lives of societies and individuals. A revelation in a gallery. A cataclysmic fire, and a salvaged notebook. Zuboff argues that we are now at one more crux point: "The age of surveillance capitalism is a titanic struggle between capital and each one of us. It is a direct intervention into free will, an assault on human autonomy." It is the capture of our intimate personal details, even of our faces. "They have no right to my face, to take it when I walk down the street."

Such violations threaten our freedom, Zuboff says. "When we think about free will, philosophers talk about closing the gap between present and future. We make ourselves a promise: I'll do something with that future moment—go to a meeting, make a phone call. If we are treated as a mass of 'users', to be herded and coaxed, then this promise becomes meaningless. I am a distinctive human. I have an indelible crucible of power within me… I should decide if my face becomes data, my home, my car, my voice becomes data. It should be my choice."

Born in New England in 1951, Zuboff is the daughter of a pharmacist and a homemaker. Her maternal grandfather, Max Miller, was a self-made entrepreneur, who invented the servomechanism for the vending machine. In her youth, she "did lots of growing up in Argentina, living on the Altiplano, with people who lived very simple lives." She is passionate about the natural world; her analogies often invoke farming and the rural environment. The only time she pauses mid-sentence is when a magpie with iridescent blue feathers alights beside us. "What a beautiful bird!" Zuboff tells me that at the start of the Industrial Revolution persuading farmers to work in factories was like trying to get a deer to pull a plough. It was too incongruous, they wouldn't do it. "Then after a while, the deer took the plough. There's a brief window before social amnesia sets in."

When I ask how deliberate this all was, if Mark Zuckerberg, Larry Page and Sergey Brin were just a bunch of happy tech-utopians who accidentally opened Pandora's box, she smiles wryly. "This was world-historical wealth creation." Surveillance capitalists have "many strategies to protect themselves from the law. Lobbying, political capture, other economic methods that we associate with cartelisation." They have also claimed that the internet is a new reality with different protocols; "Larry Page has said how could Google follow any law that came into being before the internet? This is propaganda." In her talk at the festival, Zuboff dismisses another proposition, that these are innovative companies that occasionally make mistakes. "Yes, like Google Nest [Google's home security system]: 'Oh we're so sorry, we put a microphone in the Nest surveillance system and we forgot! We forgot to put it in the schematic.'" (This story broke in February, and Google described its failure to put the microphone on tech specs as "an error".)

What about Zuckerberg's claims that "privacy is no longer a social norm," or the advice of Eric Schmidt (Google CEO, 2001–2011): "If you have something that you don't want anyone to know, maybe you shouldn't be doing it in the first place?" Zuboff has, of course, heard this line a thousand times. It has been repeated not only by surveillance capitalists, but also by governments advocating the mass surveillance of civilians. She is brisk in response: "I tell people, if you have nothing to hide then you are nothing. This isn't about Hayekian individuality, libertarianism—it's a historical process of individuation that has developed hand in hand with political freedom and democracy." It's also not Orwell, not Big Brother. "There's no one coming to take anyone away to the Gulag. It doesn't want to kill us. It just wants to move us in the direction of its predictions and get the data." Although, "in China we see the attempt to annex these technologies to the repressive state."

Some have also proposed that "choice architecture"—nudges and coaxes—can be societally beneficial, if used wisely. Proponents of this argument include Cass Sunstein and Richard Thaler (co-authors of *Nudge: Improving Decisions About Health, Wealth, and Happiness*). Zuboff disagrees vigorously. "Once you legitimate the ex-machina nudge it is intolerable. It is an act of power over the other—rather than educating or alerting. Nudging is paternalistic. Behavioural economists such as Thaler legitimated the nudge, empowered and increased the audacity of the surveillance capitalists. Thaler got the Nobel prize."

Why does she care so much? "I gave up a lot of time to write this book, over many years," she says. "I gave up time with my husband, my children. I gave up my health. Everything I had I gave, because I felt I was up against the clock of social amnesia, psychic numbing—people were losing their sense of astonishment." Yes, she agrees that "Snowden made a huge contribution to waking people up. The tech companies were implicated." Leaked documents showed the NSA collecting data from Yahoo, Google, Facebook and Microsoft. And the Cambridge Analytica scandal? "Carole Cadwalladr's work is heroic. And Chris Wylie [the Cambridge Analytica whistleblower] revealed that every aspect of Cambridge Analytica's operations was simply mimicking a day in the life of a surveillance capitalist." Instead of behavioural modification for commercial ends, the ends become political? Voting instead of buying? "Democracy is on the ropes in the UK, US, many other countries. Not in small measure because of the operations of surveillance capitalism."

Every time Zuboff speaks in public, she asks the audience: "What are the concerns that bring you here?" People call out words: privacy; dystopia; control; monopoly; manipulation; intrusion; exploitation; democracy; misinformation; fear; freedom; power; rebellion; slavery; resistance. Everywhere the words are virtually the same. What can be done? People object, but nothing happens. Doesn't that lead to lassitude? "Regulation," she says, firmly. "This is what the tech companies fear most. We say that markets that trade in human futures are illegal—like the slave trade was made illegal." Then we design "programs as a closed loop" and "reclaim the idea that we can have the digital without surveillance capitalism". This will require the "indignation" of citizens, journalists, scholars and law-makers. "Surveillance capitalism has had 20 years unimpeded by law. But it is very young."

The following day Zuboff is to give another speech, asking another audience: "What are the concerns that bring you here?" like a reclaimed version of that old Facebook question: "What's on your mind?"

Zuboff has now been on the road for nine months. The alternative, doing nothing and being "subsumed in unadulterated power" is not an option for her. "We are not simply users. We are much used. We have to awaken to our shared future."

# Big Tech Is a Threat to Democracy

*Chaze Vinci*

*Chaze Vinci is an undergraduate student at Stanford University studying public policy.*

Big Tech monopolies now pose an existential threat to our representative republic. This Wednesday, social media platforms Twitter and Facebook engaged in what can only be deemed as full-scale electoral interference and free speech discrimination by blocking the sharing of a publication piece from the *New York Post* containing information regarding Hunter Biden's business ties to a large Ukrainian energy company, Burisma. At the center of the scandal is a fundamental question we must ask ourselves as citizens of this democracy: Who controls the definition of truth?

For the entirety of the 21st century, Big Tech platforms have been granted a legal shield designed for internet companies under Section 230 of the Communications Decency Act of 1996. Designed for a radically different internet than what now exists, created long before the creation of Facebook, Google, Twitter and Instagram, the CDA was expressly designed to foster the growth of the early internet. Perhaps even more notable than the CDA's outdated nature, the law has clear legal loopholes that these firms have exploited for their own benefit. One such loophole arises as a result of the distinction between the definition of content "providers" (i.e. newspapers) and content "distributors" (i.e. newspaper stands). Distributors are deemed as passive channels of information and can therefore only be held responsible for the publication and distribution of content they know is illegal. As distributors, these firms can dictate any and all content on their platforms without legal repercussions.

Platforms such as Facebook have been granted immunity under these definitions from the federal government by naming them content distributors or "neutral information streams." With few repercussions in place from the federal government, tech platforms are able to decide for themselves what is and is not allowed on their platforms, concentrating power in the hands of these firms. This allows large internet companies to engage as arbiters of truth by single-handedly controlling what is allowed to be circulated throughout their digital space, and in an era where a majority of content is distributed from a handful of platforms, these firms are exercising unjust monopolistic power.

The *New York Post* scandal is a haunting example of the CDA run amok. Facebook Policy Communication Director Andy Stone, who formerly worked for the Democratic House Majority PAC, took to Twitter to outline the company's policies in regards to the sharing of the *New York Post* article, tweeting:

> While I will intentionally not link to the New York Post, I want be clear [sic] that this story is eligible to be fact checked by Facebook's third-party fact checking partners. In the meantime, we are **reducing its distribution on our platform**." (Emphasis added.)

Stone's ties to one of the leading Democratic PACs would cause anyone to raise an eye to the clear partisan nature of Facebook's communication decision. Regardless of partisan affiliation, Big Tech platforms should seek to engage in their public policy from a non-partisan lens, not censor speech that disagrees with their staff's ideological bend. Facebook's claim of what is, essentially, "due diligence" fact-checking is harmful information suppression given the looming date of the November election. The constitution guarantees a right to freedom of speech under the First Amendment, and this decision by the platforms poses clear threats to our cherished constitutional liberties.

This controversy comes from a long lineage of censorship on behalf of Big Tech giants, who have repeatedly sought to remove content deemed as "misinformation." While the publication of truthful information is vital to our democratic infrastructure, the issue arises in who gets to define "misinformation" and truth. For the better part of this century, Big Tech platforms have reigned supreme jurisdiction over "truth" by being able to censor content they deem to be harmful. In our democracy, the people should have access to a variety of information and decide for themselves what's truthful and what isn't. To make a wide-ranging decision such as this is to tell the American public they are incapable of thinking for themselves.

This comes at a critical moment in our democracy; there are only weeks until elections take place up and down the ballot across the country. In a case such as this one, the impact of this discretion is two-fold. Not only is this an assault on freedom of speech, but it is also a form of election interference.

The *New York Post* story has spurred leaders in Congress on both sides of the aisle to action. Senator Ted Cruz took to Twitter to criticize Twitter's actions and is calling for the CEOs of both companies—Mark Zuckerberg and Jack Dorsey, respectively— to testify in the Senate Judiciary Committee the nature of their company's election policies. Cruz has asserted that Big Tech monopolies are "drunk with power." Senator Josh Hawley, Stanford alumnus, is doing the same. Both firms will be subpoenaed in the coming days as senatorial Big Tech critics hope to hold hearings before Election Day.

The future of American democracy hangs in the balance of the coming fight against Big Tech's monopolistic practices in the digital era. This will be a battle that will define the future nature of our electoral process, our legal system, and our constitutional rights. Regardless of partisan affiliation, it's clear Big Tech's assertion of power is anything but constitutional, and it is paramount that we, as citizens, stand strong in our call for non-partisan public policy reigning in these firms.

# Big Tech Monopolies Aren't Good in the Long Run

*Shannon Bond, Alina Selyukh, and Bobby Allyn*

*Shannon Bond and Alina Selyukh are business correspondents for National Public Radio. Bobby Allyn is a business reporter for National Public Radio.*

In a sweeping report spanning 449 pages, House Democrats lay out a detailed case for stripping Apple, Amazon, Facebook and Google of the power than has made each of them dominant in their fields.

The four companies began as "scrappy underdog startups" but are now monopolies that must be restricted and regulated, the report from Democrats on the House Judiciary Committee's antitrust panel says.

"These four corporations increasingly serve as gatekeepers of commerce and communications in the digital age, and this gatekeeper power gives them enormous capacity to abuse that power," a lawyer for the subcommittee's Democratic majority said in a briefing with reporters.

The lawmakers say Congress should overhaul the laws that have let the companies grow so powerful. In particular, the report says, Congress should look at forcing "structural separations" of the companies and beefing up enforcement of existing antitrust laws.

The recommendations, if enacted, could radically change how these companies operate. They could, for example, restrict Amazon from selling its own products in its marketplace, in direct competition with sellers who depend on the platform to reach customers. Google could be banned from using the data the Android operating system collects on users and other apps to

"How Are Apple, Amazon, Facebook, Google Monopolies? House Report Counts the Ways," by Shannon Bond, Alina Selyukh, and Bobby Allyn, National Public Radio, October 6, 2020. Reprinted by permission.

refine its products. Facebook could, theoretically, be barred from acquiring another competitor, after concerns over how it bought rivals including Instagram and WhatsApp.

While the investigation was a bipartisan effort by the subcommittee, the final report has been met by partisan division over its recommendations. The Democratic majority staff authored the report, and no Republicans have publicly endorsed it so far.

Rep. Jim Jordan, R-Ohio, the ranking Republican on the Judiciary committee, was quick to dismiss the report.

"Big tech is out to get conservatives," he said in a statement, repeating a frequent but unsupported claim by conservatives. "Unfortunately, the Democrats' partisan report ignores this fundamental problem and potential solutions and instead advances radical proposals that would refashion antitrust law in the vision of the far left."

Rep. Ken Buck, R-Colo., released his own suggestions for tacking tech's power., saying he did not support the report's recommendations. But he said he agreed that Big Tech has grown too big and would work with the subcommittee's Democratic leadership to find solutions.

"An ounce of prevention is worth a pound of cure—I would rather see targeted antitrust enforcement over onerous and burdensome regulation that kills industry innovation," Buck said in a statement.

Democrats say they expect the subcommittee to vote on the report after the House recess.

The report is the culmination of a 16-month long investigation into some of the most valuable and influential companies in the world. Regardless of its uncertain political future and broad recommendations, the report presents a new and fairly comprehensive public database of evidence and internal documents that shed light on long-standing criticisms of Big Tech.

One lawyer for the antitrust subcommittee said one of the most eye-opening discoveries was the fear expressed by Fortune

500 companies in dealing with the tech giants, feeling dependent on their whims.

The tech companies are facing other investigations by federal regulators, state attorneys general and European authorities.

Here are the report's key claims about each company:

## Amazon

The report says plainly that "Amazon is the dominant online marketplace" and that evidence "demonstrates that Amazon functions as a gatekeeper for ecommerce."

Investigators detail Amazon's difficult relationship with other sellers on the platform, which it says "live in fear of the company" and which Amazon refers to as "internal competitors."

It describes sellers as "exploited" by the company's dominance: not allowed to contact shoppers directly, often limited in their ability to sell on other platforms, facing "strong-arm tactics in negotiations" and receiving either "atrocious levels of customer service" or better service for a fee.

The authors also write that Amazon profits off ideas and products developed by others, whether that's sellers on its platform, startups it considers buying or even open-source cloud-software developers.

Amazon on Tuesday published a blog post, rebutting "fallacies... at the core of regulatory spit-balling on antitrust." Without directly calling out the report, the post said: "For consumers, the result would be less choice and higher prices. Far from enhancing competition, these uninformed notions would instead reduce it."

## Apple

The report says Apple exerts "monopoly power" in the mobile app store market by favoring its own apps and disadvantaging rivals.

That dominance hurts innovation and increases prices and choices for consumers, House investigators found.

Apple, along with Google in its Google Play store, leaves developers with little choice for reaching consumers, the report says, adding that the arrangement leaves developers at the whims of the "arbitrary" enforcement of Apple's app guidelines.

The report found that the controversial 30% commission levied by Apple and Google has resulted in price increases on consumers. Investigators say that Apple generated billions of dollars in profit from the fees, despite costing about less than $100 million to operate.

In a statement, Apple said "we vehemently disagree" with the report's conclusions.

Apple, the most valuable company in the world, says it does not have a dominant market position in any of its business lines.

"Competition drives innovation, and innovation has always defined us at Apple," the company said. "We work tirelessly to deliver the best products to our customers, with safety and privacy at their core, and we will continue to do so."

## Facebook

The report quotes Facebook's own chief executive, Mark Zuckerberg, and other top management describing the company's strategy of buying its rivals. In one internal communication, Zuckerberg said Facebook "can likely always just buy any competitive startups."

Facebook used data to identify possible rivals and "then acquire, copy, or kill these firms," the report says. Facebook's monopoly power "is firmly entrenched and unlikely to be eroded by competitive pressure," investigators found.

The report said recent internal documents show that Facebook is now more worried about competition between its own products—like its photo-sharing app Instagram and its original namesake network—than outside rivals.

Investigators conclude that because it has so little competition, Facebook has "deteriorated" in quality, harming its users' privacy and leading to a "dramatic rise in misinformation."

Facebook said in a statement that it "compete[s] with a wide variety of services with millions, even billions, of people using them." It added that when it comes to Instagram and WhatsApp, "a strongly competitive landscape existed at the time of both acquisitions and exists today. Regulators thoroughly reviewed each deal and rightly did not see any reason to stop them at the time."

## Google

The report says Google enjoys a monopoly in search and search advertising, and its dominance is protected by its own data and deals it has struck around the world to be the default search engine in many browsers and devices. "No alternative search engine serves as a substitute," investigators said.

Google has maintained its dominant position by undermining search competitors and favoring its own content in search results, the report says.

The report also calls out how all the data Google collects on its users and competitors reinforces its dominance and allows it to make even more money from ads.

"Through linking these services together, Google increasingly functions as an ecosystem of interlocking monopolies," it says.

Google said in a statement it disagreed with the report, which it said "feature[s] outdated and inaccurate allegations from commercial rivals about search and other services." The company said the proposed remedies "would cause real harm to consumers, America's technology leadership and the U.S. economy—all for no clear gain."

# Technology Has Turned Toxic Because It Reflects Human Behavior

*Rob Howard*

*Rob Howard is a freelance writer.*

When in doubt, blame the robots. As Facebook has fallen from grace and struggled to reconcile its role in spreading propaganda and stoking political anger, the company has proposed a familiar solution:

If the algorithm has failed, let's just build a better algorithm.

It's a noble goal for the next hackathon. As a mechanism for real change, however, the focus on software misses the point.

Facebook's problems can't be solved with more data or better code. They're simply the most potent and alarming example of the fact that the internet has failed as a public forum.

Not long ago, the scientists and software developers who pioneered the World Wide Web thought it would democratize publishing and usher in a more open, educated, and thoughtful chapter of history.

But while the internet and its offshoot technologies have improved society and daily life in many ways, they have been an unmitigated disaster for the way people communicate and learn.

It feels good to blame Facebook, but the crisis is evident in every nook and cranny of the web. The internet is crawling with normal, everyday humans who transform into vicious, nihilistic psychopaths the moment they're granted even a thin veil of anonymity in a comment thread.

This was the nature of online communication in 1995, when astronomer and early-adopter Clifford Stoll lamented in *Newsweek*:

"The Internet Is Toxic Because Humans Are Toxic," by Rob Howard, Qrius, December 24, 2018. Reprinted by permission.

The cacophony more closely resembles citizens band radio, complete with handles, harassment, and anonymous threats. When most everyone shouts, few listen.

His words still ring true 23 years later.

Despite Facebook's efforts to make its platform less anonymous than its predecessors, it is painfully clear that people seem to have no problem piling on the hate when tapping away on a keyboard or phone, comfortably distant from the consequences of their words for the real person reading them many fiber-optic cables away.

Facebook, along with most of its social media counterparts, operates in part based on the Silicon Valley hypothesis that if all ideas are distributed freely, the most valuable ones will rise to the top.

Instead of validating that seemingly uncontroversial point, however, our collective experiences online have proven it wrong. The marketplace of ideas has become an environment with no barriers to transmitting vitriol to millions, largely negating the internet's egalitarian, utopian goals.

"I thought once everybody could speak freely and exchange information and ideas, the world is automatically going to be a better place," Evan Williams, a founder of Twitter, Blogger, and Medium, said in a 2017 interview with the *New York Times*. "I was wrong about that."

Perhaps we wouldn't still be defending this failed experiment if it wasn't so stunningly profitable. Facebook didn't invent advertising, but it has scaled the many flaws of that business model to an unprecedented magnitude.

The runaway financial success of highly targeted pay-per-view ads has warped software design into a competition to build the most addictive digital slot machine, masquerading as social engagement.

The longer we stay hooked, the more advertising we see, and the more eyeballs can be sold for a fraction of a penny apiece. This is why you get an email if you don't sign in for a few days.

This is why your apps throttle your notifications, slowly distributing the likes on your vacation photos over the course of minutes rather than seconds. It's an elaborate manipulation to keep you coming back for more.

It's also why Jeffrey Hammerbacher, a former Facebook engineer, pined for something more in a 2011 interview with *Businessweek*:

> The best minds of my generation are thinking about how to make people click ads…That sucks.

Like Facebook's other innovations, the advertising platform is valuable for individuals but disastrous at scale. The company's wealth of demographic and behavioral data helps small business owners find their niche audience, but it is also a gold mine for amateur propagandists.

The platform earns money from engagement—and guess which ads and articles are the most engaging? It's not the calm, thoughtful, balanced ones.

And that brings us to the news. Veteran journalists spent the web's first decade tentatively dipping their toes in the new technology, rightfully skeptical of its supposed virtues.

They felt the sting of getting scooped by fly-by-night blogs with low budgets and lower standards. Then, slowly but surely, they hopped on board. By the time Facebook became a significant source for news, the major publications knew better than to risk being left behind.

The rush of traffic from Facebook has been beneficial for the publications' bottom lines. However, that has been accompanied by an avalanche of meaningless and disorienting social feedback—a thoughtless "like," a forgotten "share"—that has pushed even the best publications toward clickbait and sensationalism.

There is no software that can force commenters to engage in respectful debate.

According to the analytics, that's what people like. The result is that writers and editors have far less leeway to focus on what they believe is valuable because the ultimate arbiter of success and prestige is the fleeting gratification of a page view. More news, faster news and trendier news paved the road to victory.

The source of this problem can't be found in a data center. The algorithm has failed because people are collectively seeking knowledge and human connection via the impersonal interface of the internet and then feeling angry and confused when they come up empty-handed.

There is no software that can force commenters to engage in respectful debate. There is no app to eliminate the immense conflicts of interest and perverse incentives of pay-per-view advertising sales.

There is no subroutine to stop news organizations from competing in a race to the editorial bottom, seduced by clickbait and lusting for attention at any cost.

No matter how well we code, no matter how convincingly we simulate and augment reality, our brains and bodies still know that what we experience on a screen is—in an important but ambiguous way—not real.

The people aren't really there, so we hate them. The approval isn't real, so it's never truly satisfying. And if we manage to make a friend online, we can't help but fantasize about how different it might be to meet IRL. (Yes, that's an acronym for "in real life.")

Tweak the algorithm all you want. It will never be a worthy substitute for a good book, a healthy debate, or an honest friendship. As long as we trust software to shape our interaction with the world, life will be a disappointing, chaotic, infinite scroll.

# Technology Provided Positive Benefits During the Pandemic

*Giuseppe Riva, Fabrizia Mantovani, and Brenda K. Wiederhold*

*Giuseppe Riva is in the Department of Psychology at the Università Cattolica del Sacro Cuore, Milan, Italy. Fabrizia Mantovani works in the Department of Human Sciences for Education "Riccardo Massa," University of Milano Bicocca in Milan, Italy. Brenda K. Wiederhold is from the Virtual Reality Medical Center in La Jolla, California.*

The past 10 years have seen the development and maturation of several digital technologies that can have a critical role to enhancement of happiness and psychological well-being. In particular, the past decade has seen the emergence of a new paradigm: "Positive Technology"[1-6] that can be described as the scientific and applied approach to the use of technology for improving the quality of our personal experience. The foundations of this vision come from the "Positive Psychology" approach,[7-10] a growing discipline whose main aim is to understand human strengths and virtues, and to elevate these strengths to allow individuals, groups, and societies to flourish.[11-13]

In these months the world is facing a complex crisis generated by the outbreak of a novel coronavirus-caused respiratory disease (COVID-19).[14] The impact of COVID-19 is huge. The health crisis—19,266,340 cases in 215 countries, with >717,792 deaths as of August 7, 2020 (https://www.worldometers.info/coronavirus/)—is matched by the worst economic crisis since World War II.[15] This dramatic situation is producing a significant effect on personal and social well-being. A study evaluating the psychological impact of the initial outbreak of COVID-19[16] found that 54 percent of the sample rated the psychological impact of the pandemic as moderate or severe; 17 percent declared moderate to severe depressive symptoms; 29 percent reported moderate to severe anxiety symptoms, and 8 percent reported moderate to severe stress levels. These negative psychological effects are now further aggravated by living in quarantine with its restrictions on movement and social interaction, the difficulties in obtaining basic supplies (e.g., food), and the interruption of professional activities with the subsequent financial loss.[17]

How can these problems be tackled? Different countries have opened call centers and online platforms to provide psychological counseling services for patients, their family members, and other people affected by the epidemic.[18–20] However, the organization and management of these psychological interventions have several problems that limit their efficacy.[18] First, patients are not differentiated according to the severity of their situation and often do not find appropriate department or professionals for timely and reasonable diagnosis and treatment. Moreover, the focus of these interventions is for the short term only, with poor followup for treatments and evaluations. Finally, only severe/acute cases obtain psychological interventions, even if the psychological burden of the pandemic has reached the majority of the population.

[...]

To reach this goal, three different types of technologies can be used:

- Hedonic: Technologies used to induce positive and pleasant experiences
- Eudaimonic: Technologies used to support individuals in reaching engaging and self-actualizing experiences
- Social/Interpersonal: Technologies used to support and improve social integration and/or connectedness between individuals, groups, and organizations.

[...]

## Hedonic Technologies: Using Technology to Foster Positive Emotional States

The first dimension of Positive Technology concerns how to use technology to foster positive emotional states. The model of emotions developed by Russell[22] provides a possible path for reaching this goal: the manipulation of "core affect," a neurophysiological category corresponding to the combination of valence and arousal levels that endow the subjects with a "core knowledge" about the emotional features of their experience. Simply put, a positive emotion is achieved by increasing the valence (positive) and arousal (high) of core affect (affect regulation) and by attributing this change to the contents of the proposed experience (object).

Key arguments for the usefulness of positive emotions in increasing well-being have been provided by Fredrickson[9,23] in her "broaden-and-build model" of positive emotions. According to Fredrickson, positive emotions provide the organism with nonspecific action tendencies that can lead to adaptive behavior.[9] For example, in adults, positive emotions make them more likely to interact with others, provide help to others in need, and engage in creative challenges. Moreover, by broadening an individual›s awareness and thought–action repertoire, they build upon the resultant learning to create future physical, psychological, and social resources.[23]

Several studies have shown that Virtual Reality (VR) represents a highly specialized and effective tool for the induction and the regulation of emotions in both clinical[24] and nonclinical subjects.[25] In fact, VR can be described as an *advanced imaginal system*: an experiential form of imagery that is as effective as reality at inducing emotional responses.[26–28] This feature of VR makes it the perfect tool for stress management applications aimed both to post-traumatic stress and to the generalized stress induced by the pandemic.

An example of this use of VR is the Italian virtual reality for psychological support to health care practitioners involved in the COVID-19 crisis (MIND-VR) project (www.mind-vr.com), aimed at designing, developing, and testing an advanced solution based on the use of VR for the prevention and treatment of stress-related psychopathological symptoms and post-traumatic stress disorder in hospital health care personnel involved in the COVID-19 emergency.[20] In particular, the main goal of MIND-VR is the development of different virtual environments to offer basic education on stress and anxiety and to promote relaxation.

Another possible approach is the use of "mHealth", the practice of medicine and public health supported by mobile devices. Although there is no conclusive evidence supporting the efficacy of mHealth interventions, a recent meta-analysis study of 66 randomized controlled trials has confirmed the efficacy of app-supported smartphone interventions on stress, anxiety, depression, and perceived well-being.[29]

Different apps—*Virtual Hope Box, Breathe-to-Relax, Calm,* and *Headspace*—developed by reliable sources such as the U.S. Department of Defense and university-based researchers have been suggested to help patients manage anxiety and stress related to the COVID-19 outbreak.[30] For example, *Virtual Hope Box,* an app developed by the U.S. Department of Defense, includes breathing exercises, deep muscle relaxation, and guided meditation that can help nonclinical populations to address the generalized stress induced by the pandemic.

## Eudaimonic Technologies: Using Technology to Promote Engagement and Self-Empowerment

The second level of Positive Technology is strictly related to the eudaimonic concept of well-being, and consists of investigating how technologies can be used to support individuals in reaching engaging and self-actualizing experiences.

The theory of Flow, developed by Positive Psychology pioneer Csikszentmihalyi,[31] provides a useful framework for addressing this challenge. "Flow" or "Optimal Experience" is a positive and complex state of consciousness that is present when individuals act with total involvement. The basic feature of this experience is the perceived balance between high environmental opportunities for action (challenges) and adequate personal resources in facing them (skills).

As underlined by Positive Psychology,[32,33] to cope with dramatic changes in daily life and to access new environmental opportunities for action, individuals may develop a strategy defined as "Transformation of Flow"[34]: the ability of the subject to use Flow for identifying and exploiting new and unexpected resources and sources of involvement. A specific optimal experience that is connected to the Transformation of Flow is the emotional response of Awe.[35,36] In fact, Awe consists of two central features[35,36]—(a) a need for accommodation following the (b) perception of vastness—that can induce a significant reorganization of the predictive/simulative mechanisms of the brain:

- Perception of Vastness: An update of the predictive coding given the mismatch with current representations of others,[35,36] the world, and ourselves,[37] at the base of social order maintenance[35,36]
- Need for Accommodation: The tension arising from the mismatch can translate into a drastic update of the predictive coding to accommodate unexpected experiences.[35,36]

A clearer picture of the complex relationship among awe and brain activity was recently provided by a recent voxel-based morphometry study. As demonstrated by Guan et al.[35] awe involves multiple brain regions associated with cognitive conflict control, attention, conscious self-regulation, and socioemotional regulation, suggesting its potential role in adjusting/improving their functioning.

In this view, awe-inducing technological experiences may be used to induce Transformation of Flow. Among the different types of interactive technologies investigated thus far, VR is considered the most capable of supporting the emergence of both Flow and Awe experiences.[34,38–40]

The proposed approach is the following[41]: first, to identify a possible experience that contains functional real-world demands; second, using VR for producing the experience and inducing Awe;

third, allowing cultivation, by linking the Awe experience to the actual experience of the subject. The expected effect is a functional reorganization of the brain produced by the broadening of the thought–action repertoire associated with improved self-esteem and self-efficacy.

A practical example of this approach is provided by the free COVID Feel Good (www.covidfeelgood.com) weekly self-help virtual reality protocol.[42,43] The protocol consists on watching, for a week, at least once a day, a 10-minute VR video, named "The Secret Garden," currently available in eight different languages: English, Spanish, French, Brasilian Portuguese, Italian, Catalan, Korean, and Japanese.

Subjects need to watch the video using virtual reality glasses. Then, they need to follow a series of social exercises provided on the project's website, with specific goals for each day of the week.

- Day 1: To prevent individuals from becoming obsessed with coronavirus
- Day 2: To increase self-esteem
- Day 3: To work on autobiographical memory (who we are and what we want)
- Day 4: To wake up the sense of community so subjects do not feel alone
- Day 5: To take back dreams and goals individuals had before the lockdown started
- Day 6: To work on empathy
- Day 7: To plan a long-term change.

All the exercises are designed to be experienced with another person (not necessarily physically together), to facilitate a process of critical examination and eventual revision of core assumptions and beliefs related to personal identity, relationships, and goals. Specifically, by facilitating self-reflectiveness and constructive exchange with relevant others, the protocol seeks to improve the ability to adapt to the challenges provided by the pandemic.

## Social Technologies: Using Technology to Promote Social Integration and Connectedness

The final level of Positive Technology—the social and interpersonal one—is concerned with the use of technologies to support and improve the connectedness between individuals, groups, and organizations. However, an open challenge is to understand how to use technology to create a mutual sense of awareness, which is essential to the feeling that other participants are there, and to create a strong sense of community at a distance.

As noted by Wiederhold,[44,45] the coronavirus disease pushed many individuals to shift their work and social lives online. On one side, social media are becoming the most used information tool in disasters such as the current COVID-19 pandemic. On the other side, videoconferencing technologies such as Zoom, Meet, Teams, and WebEx have made it possible to continue some social interaction during quarantine, allowing people to move their lives online while maintaining physical distance to stop the spread of the virus.

However, this process has not been straightforward, and can generate more problems than solutions.

First, an important source of anxiety is the wealth of information that social media provides.[45] According to the World Health Organization (WHO) social media are generating an infodemic, "an overabundance of information—some accurate and some not—that makes it hard for people to find trustworthy sources and reliable guidance when they need it."[45] Moreover, the increasing use of video calls and meetings is generating a new phenomenon: tiredness, anxiety, or worry resulting from overusing virtual videoconferencing platforms.[44] This technological exhaustion is generated by the technological shortcomings of video calls—delays, lack of eye contact, limited nonverbal cues—that take so much more out of a person than meeting face to face.

How can Positive Technology help in tackling these problems?

One way to overcome technological exhaustion is actually through the use of different technology. Facebook IQ commissioned a study by Neurons, Inc., to compare how 60 participants in the United

States responded both cognitively and emotionally—all participants wore EEG headsets to analyze their brain signals and measure their level of comfort and engagement—to conversing in virtual reality versus having a conversation face to face.[46] During the experience individuals met in a virtual conference room appearing as full body avatars: they can fist bump or shake hands and interact with others in ways that make for an experience that is more similar to face-to-face meetings. The results suggest that participants—especially introverts—responded positively to meeting in virtual reality and were able to establish authentic relationships within the virtual environment. As reported by one of the participants of the study[46]: "It was a lot deeper, and enjoyable, and closer to life than I expected. We moved from two strangers having the same (superficial) conversation to two humans revealing themselves and their experience of life." In line with these results several companies have developed and/or recently released different VR social platforms: Facebook Horizon (https://www.oculus.com/facebook-horizon/), VIVE Sync (https://sync.vive.com/login), AltspaceVR (https://altvr.com/), Spatial (https://spatial.io/), and VRChat (https://vrchat.com/).

Multiple researchers have underlined the importance of human values, and the extent to which they are shared by fellow citizens, for tackling the COVID-19 crisis.[47] In particular, the awareness that fellow citizens share one›s values has been found to elicit a sense of connectedness that may be crucial in promoting collective efforts to contain the pandemic. In this view, technologies that promote online exchanges among individuals across society may also be beneficial for eliciting this sense of connectedness. For example, an international social sharing platform such as "My Country Talks" (https://www.mycountrytalks.org/) provides a digital place where to set up one-on-one discussions between people with similar or different viewpoints.

Moreover, M-health offers different tools to improve social connectedness. Banskota et al.[48] identified 15 smartphone Apps that can be used to reduce older adults› isolation. These apps—that range from classical social networking apps such as Facetime and Skype, to apps for visual and hearing impairment such as Be My Eyes—address physical and cognitive limitations and have the potential to improve the quality of life of older adults, especially during social distancing or self-quarantine.

Finally, video games, too, can be used to improve social integration and connectedness. As underlined by a recent review,[49] video games allow individuals to connect through play, which is an important source of psychological well-being throughout the lifespan. This feature, combined with the different facets of in-game socialization (i.e., reduced stress, depression, and sense of loneliness) makes video games an important tool for mitigating some of the negative impacts of COVID-19 for adults and children. But the positive potential of video games is broader than this.

First exergames, allowing physical exercise and dance, are important for both maintaining physical fitness and establishing long-term adherence to exercise during the quarantine.[50] Exergames can also easily be shared with peers and families in social isolation situations becoming a tool for establishing social bonds and collective intentions. Second, video games provide a powerful medium for understanding complex situations, such as the pandemic itself or the fake news associated with it.[51] For example, Factitious (http://factitious.augamestudio.com/) is a simple game that asks players to read a small article and then decide if it is real or fake news.[52] Factitious tries to help players think more critically about fake news by providing contents that make users think critically about the content and the source. The game, by design, aims at the gray area between fake and real news to encourage players to not only think critically, but also practice the work of distinguishing between the two types of content. The new pandemic edition of the game (http://factitious-pandemic.augamestudio.com/) is now specifically targeting the infodemic generated by social media helping individuals to understand what is right and what is wrong. Another interesting example is Plague Inc: Evolved (https://www.ndemiccreations.com/en/25-plague-inc-evolved), which is a real-time strategy simulation video game that allows players to find out more about how viral diseases spread and to understand the complexities of viral outbreaks.

## Conclusions

Although the attention of the governments is still focused on the global health emergency produced by the COVID-19 pandemic, individuals are also experiencing extreme psychological stress that is producing a significant burden on our identity and relationships. In this article we discussed the potential of "Positive Technology," the scientific and applied approach to the use of technology for improving the quality of our personal experience, to augment and enhance the existing strategies for generating psychological well-being. In particular m-Health and smartphone apps, stand-alone and social virtual reality, video games, exergames, and social technologies have the potential of enhancing different critical features of our personal experience—affective quality, engagement/actualization, and connectedness—that are challenged by the pandemic and its social and economic effects.

In conclusion, as the saying goes, "a crisis provides an opportunity"; the COVID-19 pandemic provides a great opportunity for promoting and disseminating positive technologies. The *immediate availability* and successful use of positive technologies to tackle a major global societal challenge may serve to increase the public and governmental acceptance of such technologies for other areas of health care and well-being.

### Endnotes

1. Wiederhold BK, Riva G. Positive technology supports shift to preventive, integrative health. Cyberpsychology, Behavior and Social Networking 2012; 15:67–68.

2. Riva G. Personal experience in positive psychology may offer a new focus for a growing discipline. American Psychologist 2012; 67:574–575.

3. Riva G, Banos RM, Botella C, et al. Positive technology: using interactive technologies to promote positive functioning. Cyberpsychology, Behavior and Social Networking 2012; 15:69–77. Link,

4. Villani D, Cipresso P, Gaggioli A, et al. (2016) Integrating technology in positive psychology practice. Hershey, PA: IGI-Global.

5. Riva G, Wiederhold BK, Di Lernia D, et al. Virtual reality meets artificial intelligence: the emergence of advanced digital therapeutics and digital biomarkers. Annual Review of CyberTherapy and Telemedicine 2019; 18:3–7.

6. Gaggioli A, Riva G. Psychological treatments: smart tools boost mental-health care. Nature 2014; 512:28.

7. Inghilleri P, Riva G, Riva E. (2015) Introduction: Positive change in global world: Creative individuals and complex societies. In: Inghilleri PRiva GRiva E, eds. Enabling positive change flow and complexity in daily experience. Berlin: De Gruyter Open, pp. 1–5.

8. Seligman MEP, Csikszentmihalyi M. Positive psychology. American Psychologist 2000; 55:5–14.

9. Fredrickson BL. The role of positive emotions in positive psychology. The broaden-and-build theory of positive emotions. Am Psychol 2001; 56:218–226.

10. Seligman MEP. (2002) Authentic happiness: using the new positive psychology to realize your potential for lasting fulfillment. New York: Free Press.

11. Riva E, Freire T, Bassi M. (2016) The flow experience in clinical settings: applications in psychotherapy and mental health rehabilitation. In: Harmat LØrsted Andersen FUllén FWright JSadlo G, eds. Flow experience. Cham: Springer, pp. 309–326.

12. Gaggioli A, Chirico A, Triberti S, et al. Transformative interactions: designing positive technologies to foster self-transcendence and meaning. Annual Review of CyberTherapy and Telemedicine 2016; 14:169–173.

13. Riva E, Rainisio N, Boffi M. (2014) Positive change in clinical settings: flow experience in psychodynamic therapies. In: Inghilleri PRiva GRiva E, eds. Enabling positive change: flow and complexity in daily experience. Berlin: De Gruyter Open, pp. 74–90.

14. Huang C, Wang Y, Li X, et al. Clinical features of patients infected with 2019 novel coronavirus in Wuhan, China. The Lancet 2020; 395:497–506.

15. Nicola M, Alsafi Z, Sohrabi C, et al. The socio-economic implications of the coronavirus pandemic (COVID-19): a review. International Journal of Surgery 2020; 78:185–193.

16. Wang C, Pan R, Wan X, et al. Immediate Psychological Responses and Associated Factors during the Initial Stage of the 2019 Coronavirus Disease (COVID-19) Epidemic among the General Population in China. Int J Env Res Pub He 2020; 17:1729.

17. Brooks SK, Webster RK, Smith LE, et al. The psychological impact of quarantine and how to reduce it: rapid review of the evidence. The Lancet 2020; 395:912–920.

18. Duan L, Zhu G. Psychological interventions for people affected by the COVID-19 epidemic. The Lancet Psychiatry 2020; 7:300–302.

20. Imperatori C, Dakanalis A, Farina B, et al. Global Storm of Stress-Related Psychopathological Symptoms: a brief overview on the usefulness of virtual reality in facing the mental health impact of COVID-19. Cyberpsychology, Behavior, and Social Networking 2020. [Epub ahead of print]; DOI: 10.1089/cyber.2020.0339.

22. Russell JA. Core Affect and the psychological construction of Emotion. Psychological Review 2003; 110:145–172.

23. Fredrickson BL. The broaden-and-build theory of positive emotions. Philosophical Transactions of the Royal Society of London Series B, Biological Sciences 2004; 359:1367–1378.

24. Carl E, Stein AT, Levihn-Coon A, et al. Virtual reality exposure therapy for anxiety and related disorders: a meta-analysis of randomized controlled trials. Journal of Anxiety Disorders 2019; 61:27–36.

25. Hadley W, Houck C, Brown LK, et al. Moving beyond role-play: evaluating the use of virtual reality to teach emotion regulation for the prevention of adolescent risk behavior within a randomized pilot trial. Journal of Pediatric Psychology 2018; 44:425–435.

26. North MM, North SM, Coble JR. Virtual reality therapy: an effective treatment for psychological disorders. Studies in Health Technology and Informatics 1997; 44:59–70.

27. Vincelli F. From imagination to virtual reality: the future of clinical psychology. CyberPsychology & Behavior 1999; 2:241–248. Link,

28. Vincelli F, Molinari E, Riva G. Virtual reality as clinical tool: immersion and three-dimensionality in the relationship between patient and therapist. Studies in Health Technology and Informatics 2001; 81:551–553.

29. Linardon J, Cuijpers P, Carlbring P, et al. The efficacy of app-supported smartphone interventions for mental health problems: a meta-analysis of randomized controlled trials. World Psychiatry 2019; 18:325–336.

30. Wright JH, Caudill R. Remote treatment delivery in response to the COVID-19 pandemic. Psychotherapy and Psychosomatics 2020; 89:1.

31. Csikszentmihalyi M. (1990) Flow: The psychology of optimal experience. New York: HarperCollins.

32. Delle Fave A. (1996) Il processo di trasformazione di Flow in un campione di soggetti medullolesi [The process of flow transformation in a sample of subjects with spinal cord injuries]. In: Massimini FDelle Fave AInghilleri P, eds. La selezione psicologica umana. Milan: Cooperativa Libraria IULM, pp. 615–634.

33. Delle Fave A, Massimini F, Bassi M. (2011) Psychological selection and optimal experience across cultures: social empowerment through personal growth. New York: Springer.

34. Riva G, Castelnuovo G, Mantovani F. Transformation of flow in rehabilitation: the role of advanced communication technologies. Behavior Research Methods 2006; 38:237–244.

35. Guan F, Xiang Y, Chen O, et al. Neural basis of dispositional awe. Frontiers in Behavioral Neuroscience 2018; 12:209.

36. Bai Y, Maruskin LA, Chen S, et al. Awe, the diminished self, and collective engagement: universals and cultural variations in the small self. Journal of Personality and Social Psychology 2017; 113:185–209.

37. Newen A. The embodied self, the pattern theory of self, and the predictive mind. Frontiers in Psychology 2018; 9:2270.

38. Riva G, Raspelli S, Algeri D, et al. Interreality in practice: bridging virtual and real worlds in the treatment of posttraumatic stress disorders. Cyberpsychology, Behavior and Social Networking 2010; 13:55–65. Link,

39. Gaggioli A, Bassi M, Delle Fave A. (2003) Quality of experience in virtual environments. In: Riva GIJsselsteijn WADavide F, eds. Being there: concepts, effects and measurement of user presence in synthetic environment. Amsterdam: Ios Press, pp. 121–135.

40. Chirico A, Cipresso P, Yaden DB, et al. Effectiveness of immersive videos in inducing awe: an experimental study. Sci Rep 2017; 7:1218.

41. Riva G, Wiederhold B, Chirico A, et al. Brain and virtual reality: what do they have in common and how to exploit their potential. Annual Review of CyberTherapy and Telemedicine 2018; 16:3–7.

42. Riva G, Wiederhold BK. How cyberpsychology and virtual reality can help us to overcome the psychological burden of coronavirus. Cyberpsychology, Behavior & Social Networking 2020; 5:227–229.

43. Riva G, Bernardelli L, Browning MHEM, et al. COVID feel good—an easy self-help virtual reality protocol to overcome the psychological burden of coronavirus. PsyArXiv 2020. DOI: 10.31234/osf.io/6umvn.

44. Wiederhold BK. Connecting through technology during the coronavirus disease 2019 pandemic: avoiding "Zoom Fatigue." Cyberpsychology, Behavior, and Social Networking 2020; 23:437–438. Link,

45. Wiederhold BK. Using social media to our advantage: alleviating anxiety during a pandemic. Cyberpsychology, Behavior, and Social Networking 2020; 23:197–198. Link,

46. Facebook IQ. (2017) How Virtual Reality Facilitates Social Connection. https://www.facebook.com/business/news/insights/how-virtual-reality-facilitates-social-connection (accessed on Aug. 14, 2020).

47. Wolf LJ, Haddock G, Manstead ASR, et al. The importance of (shared) human values for containing the COVID-19 pandemic. Brit J Soc Psychol 2020; 59:618–627.

48. Banskota S, Healy M, Goldberg EM. 15 Smartphone apps for older adults to use while in isolation during the COVID-19 pandemic. West J Emerg Med 2020; 21:514–525.

49. Marston H, Kowert R. What role can videogames play in the COVID-19 pandemic? Emerald Open Research 2020; 2:34.

50. Viana RB, de Lira CAB. Exergames as coping strategies for anxiety disorders during the COVID-19 quarantine period. Games for Health Journal 2020; 9:147–149. Link,

51. Kriz WC. Gaming in the time of COVID-19. Simulation & Gaming 2020; 51:403–410.

52. Grace L, Hone B. (2019) Factitious: large scale computer game to fight fake news and improve news literacy. Extended Abstracts of the 2019 CHI Conference on Human Factors in Computing Systems. New York: ACM, pp. 1–8.

# Big Tech Can Promote Trust and Democracy

*Barbara Romzek and Aram Sinnreich*

*Barbara Romzek is a professor of public administration and policy at the American University School of Public Affairs. Aram Sinnreich is an associate professor of communication studies at American University's School of Communication.*

Social media websites and online services, created to profit from connecting people and encouraging global conversations, have a deep and troubling dark side. Malicious users have exploited these forums for free speech in ways that weaken shared norms of civility, trust and openness. This includes not just bullying and shaming of individuals, but also dealing significant damage to society as a whole.

Americans—and people around the world—will spend much of 2018 discussing how to handle the problem of Facebook, Twitter, Google and their ilk reaping massive profits while threatening democracy and undermining trust in public discourse. As scholars of public accountability and digital media systems, we suggest these companies could find a new way to compete that promotes trust and accuracy, bringing both private profits and public benefits.

## Social Media's Original Sin

Many problems have arisen because of how social media companies began, and how their power has grown in society. Like most Silicon Valley startups, Google, Facebook and Twitter were incubated in a libertarian, free market environment. These conditions reward people and companies who best provide powerful and convenient ways for people around the world to connect. Yet, they are engineered for the benefit of their private stockholders, not their public stakeholders.

"Social Media Companies Should Ditch Clickbait, and Compete over Trustworthiness," by Barbara Romzek and Aram Sinnreich, The Conversation, January 1, 2018, https://theconversation.com/social-media-companies-should-ditch-clickbait-and-compete-over-trustworthiness-88827. Licensed under CC BY-ND 4.0.

From Google's search algorithm to Facebook's news feed algorithm, the processes that shape our online experience are not only complex and secretive, they are intentionally opaque. That is, in fact, their primary business model.

Think about it: If everyone knew exactly how Google's algorithms worked, then unscrupulous websites could hack their way to the top of search listings, rather than earning a high ranking by improving their products and services— or by paying Google for their ads to appear alongside search results. Similarly, if Facebook revealed the method by which it selects items to appear on users' news feeds, brands and content providers would no longer need to pay the company tens of billions of dollars per year to reach their own customers on the platform.

These companies have become massive, with billions of users spending hours a day on their systems. Business is booming— but their lack of transparency and accountability is increasingly understood as a threat to civil society.

## Polluting the Public Sphere

The erosion of civility, trust and respect for truth in US society is what economists call a "negative externality." That is a cost of a product or service that is paid by society at large, rather than the company that supplies it or the customer who buys it. A common example is industrial pollution, when manufacturing companies don't pay the costs of health and environmental problems that their plants' pollution causes.

Social media companies earn extraordinary profits by collecting personal information and selling ads targeted with algorithms. This has allowed the rise of new kinds of social pollution: fake news, purposely divisive messages distributed by fake identities—even the creation of real-world political events based on these false and anti-social messages.

Just as society expects oil companies to take moral and legal responsibility for environmental pollution if they spill in the oceans and aquifers, we believe social media companies must help fix and fight the social pollution that their platforms have enabled.

## Accountability and Transparency Are Key

In our view, social media companies need to move beyond their "free market" foundations. Like any other set of institutions essential to our social infrastructures and economies, they should develop methods to provide the transparency and public accountability necessary to address the social ills their platforms have enabled.

Transparency is the best way to drive out hate speech and fake news. Without it, customers won't have confidence in the quality of the information they receive, or the goodwill of information providers. Social media companies need to be more responsive to the needs of society as a whole, and accept responsibility for monitoring the integrity of their own platforms. They must be held publicly accountable for their platforms' capacity to be used in ways that undermine our civil society and political institutions.

This is not a simple proposition, nor a change that social media platforms can make with a mere flip of a switch. But in our view, it's necessary.

Facebook has begun this process, allowing users to identify all ads a particular page buys across the site, regardless of how the ads were micro-targeted. Twitter has taken similar steps. But these are only initial efforts in what should be a much longer process.

## A New Business Opportunity

If these companies don't change, the very societies that provide their economic lifeblood will diminish and fail. Reform is in their own interest—and everyone else's too.

In the short term, social media companies should make their algorithms, and the data they analyze, more transparent to the public. One possibility could be developing centralized websites where people can check the sources of content and funding for advertisements. A promising approach, currently under way at some companies, involves adapting algorithms to reduce the prominence of fake news posts in users' feeds. Yet, despite their benefits, these initiatives don't fix the contradiction at the heart of social media: Their obscurity-based business models conflict directly with their increasingly central role as platforms for public discourse and the democratic process.

In the longer term, major internet companies will need to rethink their strategies entirely. This means developing business models that privilege transparency over obscurity, accessibility over secrecy, and accountability over accounting. Though this is a tall order, we propose that social media enterprises could pivot and expand into the business of verification and certification.

What does this mean, exactly? Facebook, Twitter, Google and others like them should start competing to provide the most accurate news instead of the most click-worthy, and the most trustworthy sources rather than the most sensational. Once these companies understand that maintaining a healthy public sphere pays better than aiding social pollution, they—and society as a whole—can begin to clean up the mess we've made together.

# Chapter 2

# Does Silicon Valley
Unfairly Target
Conservatives?

# Overview: Many Americans Believe That Social Media Shows Political Bias

*Emily A. Vogels, Andrew Perrin, and Monica Anderson*

*Emily A. Vogels is a research associate at Pew Research Center. Andrew Perrin is a research analyst at Pew Research Center. Monica Anderson is the associate director of research at Pew Research Center.*

Americans have complicated feelings about their relationship with big technology companies. While they have appreciated the impact of technology over recent decades and rely on these companies' products to communicate, shop and get news, many have also grown critical of the industry and have expressed concerns about the executives who run them.

This has become a particularly pointed issue in politics—with critics accusing tech firms of political bias and stifling open discussion. Amid these concerns, a Pew Research Center survey conducted in June finds that roughly three-quarters of U.S. adults say it is very (37%) or somewhat (36%) likely that social media sites intentionally censor political viewpoints that they find objectionable. Just 25% believe this is not likely the case.

Majorities in both major parties believe censorship is likely occurring, but this belief is especially common—and growing—among Republicans. Nine-in-ten Republicans and independents who lean toward the Republican Party say it's at least somewhat likely that social media platforms censor political viewpoints they find objectionable, up slightly from 85% in 2018, when the Center last asked this question.

At the same time, the idea that major technology companies back liberal views over conservative ones is far more widespread

"Most Americans Think Social Media Sites Censor Political Viewpoints," by Emily A. Vogels, Andrew Perrin, and Monica Anderson, Pew Research Center, August 19, 2020. Reprinted by permission. https://www.pewresearch.org/internet/2020/08/19/most-americans-think-social-media-sites-censor-political-viewpoints.

among Republicans. Today, 69% of Republicans and Republican leaners say major technology companies generally support the views of liberals over conservatives, compared with 25% of Democrats and Democratic leaners. Again, these sentiments among Republicans have risen slightly over the past two years.

Debates about censorship grew earlier this summer following Twitter's decision to label tweets from President Donald Trump as misleading. This prompted some of the president's supporters to charge that these platforms are censoring conservative voices.

This survey finds that the public is fairly split on whether social media companies should engage in this kind of fact-checking, but there is little public confidence that these platforms could determine which content should be flagged.

Partisanship is a key factor in views about the issue. Fully 73% of Democrats say they strongly or somewhat approve of social media companies labeling posts on their platforms from elected officials as inaccurate or misleading. On the other hand, 71% of Republicans say they at least somewhat disapprove of this practice. Republicans are also far more likely than Democrats to say they have no confidence at all that social media companies would be able to determine which posts on their platforms should be labeled as inaccurate or misleading (50% vs. 11%).

These are among the key findings of a Pew Research Center survey of 4,708 U.S. adults conducted June 16-22, 2020, using the Center's American Trends Panel.

## Views about whether social media companies should label posts on their platforms as inaccurate are sharply divided along political lines

Americans are divided over whether social media companies should label posts on their sites as inaccurate or misleading, with most being skeptical that these sites can accurately determine what content should be flagged.

Some 51% of Americans say they strongly or somewhat approve of social media companies labeling posts from elected officials on their platforms as inaccurate or misleading, while a similar share (46%) say they at least somewhat disapprove of this.

Democrats and Republicans hold contrasting views about the appropriateness of social media companies flagging inaccurate information on their platforms. Fully 73% of Democrats say they strongly or somewhat approve of social media companies labeling posts on their platforms from elected officials as inaccurate or misleading, versus 25% who disapprove.

These sentiments are nearly reversed for Republicans: 71% say they disapprove of social media companies engaging in this type of labeling, including about four-in-ten (39%) who say they strongly disapprove. Just 27% say they approve of this labeling.

Liberal Democrats stand out as being the most supportive of this practice: 85% of this group say they approve of social media companies labeling elected officials' posts as inaccurate or misleading, compared with 64% of conservative or moderate Democrats and even smaller shares of moderate or liberal Republicans and conservative Republicans (38% and 21%, respectively).

In addition to measuring public attitudes about flagging potentially misleading content from elected officials, the survey explored Americans' views about whether this practice would be acceptable to apply to posts from ordinary users.1 Some 52% of Americans say they strongly or somewhat approve of social media companies labeling posts from ordinary users on their platforms as inaccurate or misleading, while 45% disapprove.

Again, views vary widely by party. While seven-in-ten Democrats approve of these sites labeling posts from ordinary users as inaccurate or misleading, that share falls to 34% among Republicans. Americans' support—or lack thereof—for flagging content on social media is similar whether applied to posts by politicians or everyday users.

But the public as a whole does not trust that these companies will be able to decide on which posts should be labeled as misleading. Overall, a majority of Americans (66%) say they have not too much or no confidence at all in social media companies being able to determine which posts on their platforms should be labeled as inaccurate or misleading, with 31% saying they have a great deal or some confidence.

Republicans are far more likely than Democrats to express skepticism that social media companies could properly determine which posts should be labeled in this way. More than eight-in-ten Republicans say they have no (50%) or not much (34%) confidence regarding social media companies' ability to determine which posts on their platforms should be labeled.

Democrats are more evenly split in their views: Some 52% of Democrats say they have no confidence at all or not too much confidence in social media companies to determine which posts on their platforms should be labeled as inaccurate or misleading, while 46% say they have a great deal or fair amount of confidence.

Beyond that, there are notable differences along partisan and ideological lines. Six-in-ten conservative Republicans say they have no confidence in social media companies' ability to determine which posts on their platforms should be labeled as misleading, compared with 34% of moderate or liberal Republicans and 11% each of conservative or moderate Democrats and liberal Democrats.

Americans who approve of social media companies labeling posts express more confidence that these sites could properly flag inaccurate content. Indeed, 54% of those who approve of labeling elected officials' posts as misleading say they have at least a fair deal of confidence in social media companies to determine which posts to label, while only 9% of those who disapprove of labeling elected officials' posts say the same. A similar pattern is present when asked about this type of labeling for ordinary users.

The confidence gap between Republicans and Democrats remains present even among those who approve of this type of flagging. Some 56% of Democrats who approve of social media platforms labeling elected officials' posts as inaccurate say they have at least a fair amount of confidence in these companies to determine which posts to label, compared with 42% of Republicans who approve of labeling elected officials' posts as misleading or inaccurate. This partisan gap is even larger among those who approve of labeling ordinary users' posts. Roughly six-in-ten Democrats (58%) who approve of labeling ordinary users' posts express a great deal or a fair amount of confidence in social media companies to determine which posts to label, while 30% of their Republican counterparts say that.

## Majorities across parties—but particularly Republicans—say it is at least somewhat likely social media sites censor political views they find objectionable

Americans by and large believe social media companies are censoring political viewpoints they find objectionable. Roughly three-quarters of Americans (73%) think it is very or somewhat likely that social media sites intentionally censor political viewpoints they find objectionable, including 37% who say this is very likely.

Larger shares in both parties think it's likely that these sites engage in political censorship, but this belief is especially widespread among Republicans. Fully 90% of Republicans say that social media sites intentionally censor political viewpoints that they find objectionable—with 60% saying this is very likely the case. By comparison, fewer Democrats believe this to be very (19%) or somewhat (40%) likely.

Republicans—but not Democrats—are divided along ideological lines on the issue. Conservative Republicans are far more likely than moderate or liberal Republicans to say it is very likely that social media sites intentionally censor political viewpoints they find objectionable (70% vs. 44%). Similar shares of moderate or conservative Democrats (20%) and liberal Democrats (18%) express this view.

While these overall views about censorship are on par with those in 2018, there has been a slight uptick in the share of Republicans who think censorship is likely the norm on social media. Today,

90% of Republicans believe it is very or somewhat likely that social media sites intentionally censor political viewpoints—a modest yet statistically significant increase from 2018, when 85% expressed this view. The share of conservative Republicans who say this is very likely the case rose 7 points, from 63% in 2018 to 70% in 2020. Views among moderate and liberal Republicans, as well as Democrats across the ideological spectrum, have not significantly changed since 2018.

## Roughly seven-in-ten Republicans say major technology companies tend to support the views of liberals over conservatives

While most Republicans and Democrats believe it's likely that social media sites engage in censoring political viewpoints, they do diverge on which views they think major technology companies tend to favor.

On a broad level, a plurality of Americans say major technology companies tend to support the views of liberals over conservatives, rather than conservatives over liberals (43% vs. 13%). Still, about four-in-ten (39%) say major tech companies tend to support the views of conservatives and liberals equally. The share who say major technology companies equally support the views of conservatives and liberals has slightly decreased since 2018, while the other two sentiments are statistically unchanged.

Public attitudes on this issue are highly partisan. Today, 69% of Republicans say major technology companies favor the views of liberals over conservatives, while 22% say these companies support the views of liberals and conservatives equally. Few Republicans (5%) believe that conservative sentiments are valued more than liberal ones by these companies.

By comparison, one-quarter of Democrats say major technology companies support liberal views over conservative ones, while 19% say conservative sentiments are the ones that are more valued. About half of Democrats (52%) believe tech companies treat these views equally.

There are also large differences when accounting for political ideology. For example, 81% of conservative Republicans say big technology companies favor liberal views, compared with half of moderate or liberal Republicans and even smaller shares of conservative or moderate Democrats (24%) and liberal Democrats (26%).

When asked about the preference of conservative views, 23% of liberal Democrats—a slightly larger share than the 16% in 2018— say that major technology companies favor these views over liberal ones, compared with 10% or fewer of moderate to liberal and conservative Republicans.

# Democracy Suffers When Big Tech Is Biased

*Leni Friedman Valenta and Jiri Valenta*

*Leni Friedman Valenta is a graduate of Brandeis and Yale University. Jiri Valenta is an international expert and senior research associate at the Begin-Sadat Center for Strategic Studies for which they both write.*

D igital giants have been playing an increasingly significant role in wider society... how well does this monopolism correlate with the public interest?," Russian President Vladimir Putin said on January 27, 2021.

> Where is the distinction between successful global businesses, sought-after services and big data consolidation on the one hand, and the efforts to rule society[...] by substituting legitimate democratic institutions, by restricting the natural right for people to decide how to live and what view to express freely on the other hand?

Was Mr. Putin defending democracy? Hardly. What apparently worries him is that the Big Tech might gain the power to control society at the expense of his government. What must be a nightmare for him—as for many Americans—is that the Tech giants were able to censor news favorable to Trump and then censor Trump himself. How could the U.S. do this to the president of a great and free country?

Putin made these comments at the Davos World Economic Forum, in which he and Chinese President Xi Jinping, sped on by the "Great Reset" of a fourth industrial revolution, used enlightened phrases to mask dark plans for nation states in a globalist New World Order. Thus did Xi caution attendees "to adapt to and guide globalization, cushion its negative impact, and deliver its benefits to all countries and all nations."

In March 2019, Putin signed a law "imposing penalties for Russian internet users caught spread 'fake news' and information that presents 'clear disrespect for society, government, state symbols the constitution and government institutions.'" Punishments got even heavier with new laws in December.

Meanwhile, opposition leader Alexei Navalny has been sentenced to prison for more than three years (with a year off for time served), in part because he revealed photos of a lavish Russian palace allegedly belonging to Putin on the coast of the Black Sea. Its accouterments supposedly include an $824 toilet brush. Many of the thousands of people protesting Navalny's imprisonment have since been protesting Putin by waving gold-painted toilet brushes.

How nice that American Big Tech companies is pushing democracy in Russia—even while it is denying it at home. Do you notice how many leaders in Europe have risen to condemn censorship in America even though many in Europe are censoring their citizens as well, and are not exactly fans of the person who was being censored, former President Donald J. Trump? Like Putin, they probably do not want Big Tech competing with their governments, either.

The power-sharing of the U.S. Federal government with Big Tech appears a recipe for unharnessed power and corruption. Navalny caught on right away, saying:

> This precedent will be exploited by the enemies of freedom of speech around the world. In Russia as well. Every time when they need to silence someone, they will say: "this is just common practice, even Trump got blocked on Twitter."

What watchdog, if any, is now restraining Big Tech in America? It has become quite clear that Big Tech's censorship may well have cost Trump the election, even if one ultimately finds that election fraud did not.

Big Tech took it upon itself to censor an exposé—published by the *New York Post* on October 24, 2020, as well as follow-up exposés— reporting that Hunter Biden, Joe Biden's son, had sold his influence to China and Ukraine, and had raked in millions for the family.

The Media Research Center (MRC) found that "One of every six Biden voters we surveyed (17%) said they would have abandoned the Democratic candidate had they known the facts about one or more of these news stories." That information might well have changed the outcome in all six of the swing states Biden reportedly won.

Last August, Twitter also undertook censoring the trailer of an explosive documentary entitled "The Plot Against the President." The film, narrated by Rep. Devin Nunes (R-CA) with commentary by leading members of the Republican Party, exposes leading members of the Democratic Party and their deep state allies, many of whom knowingly used phony evidence to frame President Trump and some in his circle to try convince Americans that he and his campaign had colluded with the Russian government to win the 2016 election.

The film claims, using with recently declassified information, that President Barack Obama, as well Hillary Clinton, were involved in an almost four-year attempted coup incomparably more undemocratic than any riot at the Capitol Building on January 6.

Rep. Devin Nunes, the top Republican on the House Intelligence Committee, claimed in August 2020 that Biden also knew of the ongoing efforts to unseat Trump. Nevertheless, Trump did not target them, perhaps to avoid dividing the country even further.

According to the Washington Times, the Twitter account of the movie, which debuted in October 2020, attracted 30,000 followers. Twitter blacklisted it for a day, but after a public uproar, put the popular documentary back. Our question is: How many blacklistings did Twitter not put back?

The January 6 riot at the U.S. Capitol was a pivotal event for Trump and the Republican Party. Prior to January 6, President Trump had offered to deploy 10,000 troops to the capitol, according to his former Chief-of-Staff Mark Meadows. The Pentagon and the Department of Justice had also offered help but were also reportedly turned down by the US Capitol Police.

The problem, apparently, was "optics"—about a Capitol now surrounded by barbed wire and thousands of troops, which the current Administration now seems to like.

Freedom of Information Act (FOIA) requests for further details about the event were also rejected—it is not clear by whom. It is ridiculous, therefore, for anyone to frame the riots, ugly as they were, as a seditious "insurrection," particularly in light of what appears to be a massive security failure that could have averted the violence. One thing is certain: the timing of the event could not have been more perfect for opposition groups, which is probably why it had been planned for weeks before January 6.

What these efforts and the media did achieve was an end to all attempts to ascertain election fraud at a time when Vice President Mike Pence was counting Electoral College ballots, and allowing speeches from those supporting that claim. Some politicians even called for the resignation of Senators Ted Cruz and Josh Hawley, and referred them to the ethics committee for even suggesting an election audit of battleground states, despite questions having been asked—with no objections—concerning the results of the 2000, 2004 and 2016 presidential elections.

Ultimately, the result of the latest "witch hunt" against President Trump, as it has been called, was a contrived impeachment attempt to bar Trump from a future presidential bid—a kangaroo court devoid of due process, hearings, witnesses, and evidence. The prosecution, however, was undeniably eloquent in evoking "democracy" for a totally undemocratic procedure that justly resulted in Trump's acquittal.

Meanwhile, Facebook and Twitter banned Trump and some of his supporters from their cyber domains. An alternative social media platform, Parler, was banned from the Apple and Google app stores, and then completely closed down by Amazon.

Meanwhile, mainstream social media platforms were reportedly used to rally and organize carry out riots in American cities last year. No one was penalized.

Do not, however, expect such slackness now. According to Fox News:

> People like Obama-era CIA Director John Brennan and Rep. Alexandria Ocasio-Cortez, D-N.Y., have made various public statements labeling Republicans as extremists—with Ocasio-Cortez claiming the GOP has "white supremacist sympathizers' within its ranks, and Brennan claiming 'domestic violent extremists" in the

form of far-right supporters of President Trump are more dangerous than Al Qaeda.

Columnist and radio host Jeffrey Kuhner warns that a new bill, H.R. 350, "is the liberals' equivalent of the Patriot Act redux. This time, however, it is not aimed at Islamic jihadists. Rather, it directly targets Trump patriots." Kuhner writes that the bill "has the full backing of the Democratic congressional leadership, the Biden administration... Big Media and Big Tech."

> The bill empowers the Deep State to monitor, surveil and spy on American citizens' social media accounts, phone calls, political meetings and even infiltrate pro-Trump or "Stop the Steal" rallies.
> Conservatives who are deemed potentially "seditious" or "treasonous" can be arrested and jailed, fined and/or lose their employment. The goal is simple: to crush all dissent to the Biden regime.

Moreover, last month the new Secretary of Defense, Lloyd Austin, ordered a "stand down of the entire military for 60 days, so each service, each command and each unit can have a deeper conversation about this issue [extremism]." Normally stand downs last only a few hours or days and do not involve the entire military. Austin, in addition, has pledged to "rid our ranks of racists and extremists."

These are words that can be applied to anyone dreamed up, including Trump supporters, and based, of course, on nothing but propaganda.

Austin's plan is therefore needless, divisive and dangerous, considering the foreign dangers now circling their prey. This punishment of the regime's "foes" makes one wonder what is next. Are we already marching in lockstep with Russia and China? The way to unite and strengthen the United States is not through suppression and punishment but through political power with checks and balances, a free press and closer adherence to the Constitution.

But here, again, there seems to be. a problem. The Federalist wrote in July:

According to a new Quillette survey released last month, 70 percent of self-identifying liberals want to rewrite the U.S. Constitution "to a new Americans constitution that better reflects our diversity as a people."

Oh, so that is what we lack: diversity!

What can Americans Do? We are presently at a tipping point in America. Communist China is working hard and is focused on global domination; we are just messing around. In an increasingly digital world, the war against infringements on our freedoms most probably needs to be fought largely in the digital and cyber-space. That is why ending censorship in both the traditional and social media is such an important priority. First, break up the Big Tech companies. Let them become the utilities they originally claimed to be, or else be liable to lawsuits as other publishers are.

We do take some comfort that whereas dictatorships in authoritarian countries such as China and Russia is vertical—from the top down—in America, the central government shares power with the states from the bottom up, and with powers separated: the executive, the judiciary and the legislative. Fortunately, governors such as Ron DeSantis in Florida, Greg Abbott in Texas and Kevin Stitt in Oklahoma are now moving legislatively to counter federal laws that may have adverse effects on freedom of speech, jobs, election integrity, the energy industry, the first or second amendments and general constitutional rights.

This does not speak, however, to the major issue here—that democracy cannot survive in a country where a few technocrats and oligarchs can choose to deny access to information or platforms to candidates running for office. It is simply unacceptable that they alone—unelected, unappointed, untransparent and unaccountable—can deem what is "harmful" to society. The job now for all of us is to prevent the United States from slowly becoming a full-blown tyranny.

# Mainstream Media Platforms Are Being Abandoned by Conservatives

*Jason Wilson*

*Jason Wilson is an Australian-born writer for the* Guardian *who lives in Portland, Oregon.*

Following the banning of Donald Trump and many prominent followers on mainstream social media platforms, and Amazon's withdrawal of web hosting from Parler, rightwingers have fled to an archipelago of smaller "alt tech" sites and services that promise less content moderation or a refuge from the prying eyes of their political opponents and law enforcement.

On Tuesday, on Apple's App Store and Google's Play store, apps, services and social networking platforms that either directly pitch themselves to Trumpists as a free speech alternative, or which allow them to enjoy encrypted communications, were dominating the list of the most downloaded apps.

Some of these were platforms that—like the temporarily disappeared Parler—seek to reproduce some of the features of big tech platforms, but with far fewer restrictions on what users can post.

One example, CloutHub, was founded by Jeff Brain, an Irvine, California-based businessman, in 2018. It was originally pitched as a hub for civic engagement and on Brain's LinkedIn site, it is still described as giving "tools to organize, exchange information, hold meetings, create a better-informed public, increase public participation, and effectively advocate their positions."

Since last December, though, when pro-Trump "stop the steal" activists were increasingly receiving sanctions on mainstream sites, it has more squarely presented itself as a redoubt for conservatives who have been "disenfranchised by big tech."

"Rightwingers Flock to 'Alt Tech' Networks as Mainstream Sites Ban Trump," by Jason Wilson, Guardian News and Media Limited, January 13, 2021. Reprinted by permission.

It has acquired a number of high-profile "ambassadors," including the Republican party official and lawyer Harmeet Dhillon, the Hercules actor Kevin Sorbo and the pro-Trump meme peddler Logan Cook, who operates under the alias "Carpe Donktum."

CloutHub also offers a function for rightwingers missing their frenetic Facebook groups. On his own CloutHub page as of Tuesday, Brain was offering links to an anti-lockdown page demanding the reopening of houses of worship. Other groups included "Patriot's Corner," "Women for Trump," and "QAnon: The Official Group Page on CloutHub."

The site is one player among a cluster of sites like MeWe and Minds.com whose light touch in content moderation is presented as a commitment to free speech. The laissez-faire attitude of those sites has led many conservatives to at least set up accounts ahead of any bans they might receive on other platforms. On MeWe, for example, the QAnon-boosting lawyer Lin Wood, conservative broadcaster Mark Levin and Eric Trump all have profiles, but have so far posted little or no content.

A far more concerning case is Gab, founded by Andrew Torba in 2016 in response to what he called "the entirely left-leaning Big Social monopoly." It immediately attracted users associated with the "alt-right," who were beginning to come under some pressure on mainstream platforms. Gab soon developed into an echo chamber of hate speech and far-right radicalization where the Pittsburgh shooting suspect Robert Bowers announced a mass murder of worshippers at the Tree of Life synagogue.

Parler is currently down and out but it has found a new hosting company in the form of Epik, which has repeatedly stepped in to save far-right-friendly websites. If it does come back in some form, it will only be after a painful migration of its user data. It is an open question whether the security issues exposed by a data breach that has apparently struck the site will make its old users reluctant to return.

Megan Squire is a professor of computer science at Elon University and has published extensive research on the far right's use of alternative tech platforms. She says Parler's troubles are symptomatic of the difficulty of competing with established big tech players when it comes to the security of users.

"Facebook has a 16-year lead on you," she said.

She added that anyone considering using any alt tech platform should find out information about security arrangements and what was being done with their data.

Alongside the alt tech social media platforms are a number of sites that reproduce one or the other of YouTube's two most important features: the ability to post and share video, and the ability to livestream to an audience.

The video sharing sites—like Rumble and BitChute—also make their pitch to users on the basis of lax moderation. BitChute, in particular, has become home to huge amounts of neo-Nazi material, including coded death threats against journalists and activists.

The selling point of platforms like DLive is a combination of light-touch moderation and the opportunity to make money through livestreaming. Squire explains that DLive's functionality is similar to YouTube's Super Chat, in that live stream viewers can engage in cross-chat, and, importantly, offer tips to streamers in the platform's own cryptocurrency.

One prominent white nationalist streamer, Nick Fuentes, was banned from the site in the wake of the Capitol riot, which he streamed. Squire says that on average, in the year leading up to the ban, Fuentes was making an average of $418 a day, the site's blockchain records show, "and that average includes the days when he didn't stream at all."

Though his remaining holdings on the site were frozen after the ban, Fuentes drew down his earnings regularly, and had a direct financial incentive to attend the Capitol protests.

Another popular download in recent days has been Signal, an encrypted messaging application with a broad range of users. It offers the ability to send encrypted text messages and make encrypted voice calls, whether one-to-one or in groups. It is not specifically marked by the influence of the far right, nor specifically marketed to them.

The Guardian previously reported on the former Washington state representative Matt Shea's use of the app to secretly coordinate surveillance of constituents, and his followers' use of the platform to ventilate conspiracy theories and fantasies of violence.

Lastly, Telegram, which on Tuesday evening was listed as the No 2 download on both the Play store and the App Store, according to Squire represents a kind of Swiss army knife for far-right movements seeking to recruit and radicalize supporters. While she emphasizes that it, too, has a wide range of users, the majority of whom are not extremists, its hands-off approach to moderation in combination with several key features makes it irresistible to anyone unable to use mainstream services.

"It allows file storage, voice chat, and audio and video sharing," she says, meaning that a wide range of content and communication styles can be employed. It also offers one-to-many communication in channels, and many-to-many communication in chats, including encrypted chats.

But most important element is its "one-two punch," Squire says, wherein after groups "publish their outward-facing propaganda, they can draw recruits into a chat, then an encrypted chat, and further and further towards the inner circle of their group."

Radicalization on Telegram, she adds, proceeds by users being led to "peel back layers of an onion."

And this is the environment that possibly tens of thousands of disillusioned Trumpists have entered this week.

# Tech Companies Have the Right to "Censor" Conservatives and Anyone Else

*Jon Hersey*

*Jon Hersey is managing editor of* The Objective Standard, *fellow and instructor at Objective Standard Institute, and Hazlitt Fellow at Foundation for Economic Education.*

O n Monday, Florida Gov. Ron DeSantis signed a "Big Tech Bill" that he says is designed to combat Orwellian censorship by companies such as Facebook, Twitter, and Google. The law requires companies to publicly disclose their moderation policies (something most, if not all, already do) and to stick to those policies consistently. If they don't—or if users think they don't—the companies can be sued for up to $100,000 per offense.

For the past several years, everyone from Sacha Baron Cohen to Elizabeth Warren to Donald Trump has advocated for strict new regulations on tech companies, with conservatives in particular charging these companies with censorship. Is DeSantis's new law the big win for free speech that he says it is, or is it the very sort of rights violation the governor claims to be fighting?

It's no secret that tech CEOs support the political left; Mark Zuckerberg called Silicon Valley "an extremely left-leaning place." Senators Josh Hawley and Ted Cruz—along with such commentators as Dennis Prager, Ben Shapiro, Dave Rubin, Eric Weinstein, and Sam Harris—claim that the moderation practices of social-media companies demonstrate an unmistakable anti-conservative bias. And many, including DeSantis, say this bias is a form of censorship.

"If Big Tech censors enforce rules inconsistently, to discriminate in favor of the dominant Silicon Valley ideology," says DeSantis, "they will now be held accountable." He tweeted: "Florida's Big Tech Bill gives every Floridian the power to fight back against deplatforming and allows any person to sue Big Tech companies for up to $100,000 in damages. Today, we level the playing field between celebrity and citizen on social media."

There's no denying that tech companies have tremendous power over what users see on their platforms. And given that, as the Pew Research Center reports, some 72 percent of Americans use some form of social media, platforms certainly have a hand in shaping debates. So it's understandably maddening when these companies use their platforms to help one group push an agenda that many others consider destructive, promoting the content of some while "shadow-banning" others.

Thus, conservatives, seemingly the special target of "the Silicon Valley elites," as DeSantis calls them, have long been attempting to fight back against this so-called "censorship." In May 2019, President Trump tweeted: "I am continuing to monitor the censorship of AMERICAN CITIZENS on social media platforms. This is the United States of America—and we have what's known as FREEDOM OF SPEECH! We are monitoring and watching, closely!!" Six weeks later, Senator Hawley introduced a bill to amend the Communications Decency Act, revoking the legal protection that keeps social media companies from being sued for things that users post. Hawley failed to change the federal law, but DeSantis has succeeded at the state level with a more targeted set of regulations.

Tech companies have yet to respond, so we don't know whether they will play ball, oppose the law in court, or exit markets as they have in some countries, leaving users—including many businesses that rely on social media for advertising—without service. What is clear though, is that the law inserts government into the process of social-media moderation. Elected officials—beholden to their parties and constituents, always vying for re-election—will now have a hand in refereeing what is politically neutral and what is not. Is this a rational means of fighting "censorship," or is the law itself an indirect means of instituting censorship? Further, are social media companies actually censoring people by moderating the use of company property as they see fit?

Suppose you use your time and resources to build an actual wall and then invite your neighbors to graffiti it as they wish. Some are talented like Banksy, creating interesting works of art, whereas others defile it with the equivalent of fifth-grade toilet humor. Most are somewhere in between. It's your property, and you decide to paint over all of the crude stuff, plus some things you just don't like. Could this properly be called censorship? Does it violate anyone's right to free speech?

Definitely not. The reason the Founding Fathers wrote into the very first amendment that "Congress shall make no law . . . abridging the freedom of speech, or of the press" is because they understood that government has a monopoly on the legal use of force. If you don't do what the government tells you, it can take your property or put you in jail. Censorship means restrictions on speech backed by force—that is, by government.

Private companies, on the other hand, may use their property however they see fit, but they cannot force you to do anything. As I've written elsewhere,

> It's not censorship if a Christian publisher rejects an atheist's book, or if a left-leaning newspaper doesn't hire (or fires) a freedom-loving columnist, or if a Romantic art gallery refuses to display a banana duct-taped to a wall, or if a social-media platform bans Alex Jones. The right to speak one's mind is not a right to a book contract, a newspaper column, a gallery exhibit, a social-media platform, or to any product of another person's effort. A person's right to speak his mind is not a right to another person's property or support. There can be no right that violates another person's rights.

Love or hate their policies or politics, every successful tech entrepreneur started with a vision for providing value to users, then invested massive amounts of time and effort bringing that vision to life. They poured their life and property into their products and services, which they rightfully own and may use or moderate as they see fit.

If people dislike a company's policies, they have plenty of options. They are free to stop dealing with that company, to convince others to boycott it with them, to try getting a job at that company where they can advocate change from within, or to start a competing company. What they cannot rightfully do is use government power to force others to supply them with a platform moderated according to their preferences.

DeSantis is not "leveling the playing field" as he says, but rather trying to use government power to constrain how companies use their property—and, in so doing, he's carving a role for government in moderating speech. If we want a free and fair internet, we must respect the rights of tech companies, vote with our screen time— and reject DeSantis's move toward a truly Orwellian world.

# Algorithms Control What Users See on Social Media

*Steve Dempsey*

*Steve Dempsey is a columnist and the product director at INM, an Irish media organization.*

Facebook found itself in hot water recently over allegations of editorial bias. The curators of its Trending Topics feature were reportedly suppressing news from conservative media outlets. The social network responded with a charm offensive to right-wingers and a promise to "minimise risks where human judgment is involved".

Social media plays an increasingly important role in shaping people's perceptions of the world—especially when it comes to topics like politics, where polarised opinions abound. And while traditional media outlets wear their editorial biases on their sleeve, social media can be less transparent.

Many show stories to users decided by an algorithm that's designed to keep them on-site for longer. The results? Less exposure to different opinions, entrenchment of ideals and confirmation bias. It's not a list that traditional media outlets would be proud of.

A new experiment from the *Wall Street Journal* aims to show just how wide the gap is between different political persuasions on Facebook. Blue Feed Red Feed presents current stories about American politics from the most conservative-aligned and liberal-aligned sources side by side. These sources were previously uncovered by Facebook itself, in a research paper snappily entitled "Replication Data for: Exposure to Ideologically Diverse News and Opinion on Facebook."

"Steve Dempsey: 'Trust Me, I'm an Algorithm.' Presenting Polarised Opinion on Social Media," by Steve Dempsey, *Independent Ireland*, May 29, 2016. Reprinted by permission.

"Everyone thinks that we all see the same sort of thing on Facebook, while in reality everyone's feed is unique," says Jon Keegan, visual correspondent with the *Wall Street Journal*.

"I really wanted to see what sources were most popular with liberals and conservatives on Facebook—yet only Facebook can truly provide this data. When I saw Facebook's study and their replication data that included a list of the top 500 sources from their study, along with information about which groups aligned with each source, I knew I could build this side-by-side view for the first time."

These red and blue feeds aren't approximations of real news feeds as seen by liberals or conservatives. Nonetheless, Keegan was intrigued by how much the feeds differed.

"When I had my first prototype of this working, it immediately showed this really stark contrast," he says. "My editor and I quickly realised that the most interesting view of this is based around topics in the news. For example, when Bruce Springsteen decided to boycott performances in North Carolina to protest the state's transgender bathroom bill, the liberal side cheered him as a hero, while conservatives attacked him for his politics."

Keegan is keen to continue the project throughout the election and beyond, into other areas. "We'll be adding new topics throughout the rest of the election season in the US," he says. "And I could totally imagine seeing this idea used for science, sports, religion or any other topic that had passionate and potentially polarised communities. You don't want to build something just to enrage people, or to gawk at the other side—that's where you have to be careful."

The *Wall Street Journal*'s Blue Feed Red Feed project illustrates how the media has an important role to play in this age of algorithmically-driven content discovery.

"The media landscape is changing rapidly," says Keegan, "and a lot of it is intentionally designed to appear to be 'magic' to users—opaque in its design. As we've seen with Facebook's Trending Topics controversy, people do care about how this information gets to their feed, and many have called for greater transparency, which is good for everyone.

"If journalists can access data about how users are consuming and sharing information on these platforms, I think we can help the public better understand these rapidly growing businesses and the workings of this ever-changing media landscape."

Last year, the Pew Research Centre found that 61pc of American 18- to 34-year-olds now consume political news from Facebook in any given week. And the *Financial Times* reported that Facebook's "voter megaphone" feature could well be a deciding factor in the UK's EU referendum on June 23. With this much influence, it's important that someone is interrogating what social channels show their users and exposing the gaps in the feed.

Sure, traditional media outlets have become overly reliant on social networks to deliver audiences. But there's an opportunity for news publishers to become trusted advisors who help us make sense of the world as mediated by social media.

# Far-Right Views Thrive on Facebook

*Michel Martin and Will Jarvis*

*Michel Martin is a journalist and weekend host of NPR's* All Things Considered. *Will Jarvis is a journalist and news assistant at NPR.*

B y the time a pro-Trump mob stormed the U.S. Capitol on Jan. 6, fueled by far-right conspiracies and lies about a stolen election, a group of researchers at New York University had been compiling Facebook engagement data for months.

The NYU-based group, Cybersecurity For Democracy, was studying online misinformation—wanting to know how different types of news sources engaged with their audiences on Facebook. After the events of Jan. 6, researcher Laura Edelson expected to see a spike in Facebook users engaging with the day's news, similar to Election Day.

But Edelson, who helped lead the research, said her team noticed a troubling phenomenon.

"The thing was, most of that spike was concentrated among the partisan extremes and misinformation providers," Edelson told NPR's All Things Considered. "And when I really sit back and think about that, I think the idea that on a day like that, which was so scary and so uncertain, that the most extreme and least reputable sources were the ones Facebook users were engaging with, is pretty troubling."

But it wasn't just one day of high engagement. A new study from Cybersecurity For Democracy found that far-right accounts known for spreading misinformation are not only thriving on Facebook, they're actually more successful than other kinds of accounts at getting likes, shares and other forms of user engagement.

It wasn't a small edge, either.

"It's almost twice as much engagement per follower among the sources that have a reputation for spreading misinformation," Edelson

"Far-Right Misinformation Is Thriving on Facebook. A New Study Shows Just How Much," by Michel Martin and Will Jarvis, National Public Radio, March 6, 2021. Reprinted by permission.

said. "So, clearly, that portion of the news ecosystem is behaving very differently."

The research team used CrowdTangle, a Facebook-owned tool that measures engagement, to analyze more than 8 million posts from almost 3,000 news and information sources over a five-month period. Those sources were placed in one of five categories for partisanship— Far Right, Slightly Right, Center, Slightly Left, Far Left—using evaluations from Media Bias/Fact Check and NewsGuard.

Each source was then evaluated on whether it had a history of spreading misinformation or conspiracy theories. What Edelson and her colleagues discovered is what some Facebook critics—and at least one anonymous executive—have been saying for some time: that far-right content is just more engaging. In fact, the study found that among far-right sources, those known for spreading misinformation significantly outperformed non-misinformation sources.

In all other partisan categories, though, "the sources that have a reputation for spreading misinformation just don't engage as well," Edelson said. "There could be a variety of reasons for that, but certainly the simplest explanation would be that users don't find them as credible and don't want to engage with them." The researchers called this phenomenon the "misinformation penalty."

Facebook has repeatedly promised to address the spread of conspiracies and misinformation on its site. Joe Osborne, a Facebook spokesperson, told NPR in a statement that engagement is not the same as how many people actually see a piece of content. "When you look at the content that gets the most reach across Facebook, it's not at all as partisan as this study suggests," he said.

In response, Edelson called on Facebook to be transparent with how it tracks impressions and promotes content: "They can't say their data leads to a different conclusion but then not make that data public." "I think what's very clear is that Facebook has a misinformation problem," she said. "I think any system that attempts to promote the most engaging content, from what we call tell, will wind up promoting misinformation."

Editor's note: Facebook is among NPR's financial supporters.

# Texas Republicans Rail Against the Actions of Big Tech

*Duncan Agnew and Bryan Mena*

*Duncan Agnew is a student at Northwestern University and a spring intern at the* Texas Tribune. *Bryan Mena is a student at the University of Texas-El Paso and a spring reporting fellow at the* Texas Tribune.

After major technology and social media companies this month banned former President Donald Trump from their platforms and dumped conspiracy peddling accounts and the app Parler over their respective roles in inciting the deadly siege on the US Capitol, Texas Republicans portrayed the moves as discrimination against GOP voices.

But many lawmakers did so without acknowledging or decrying the role Republicans and social media played in stoking the baseless conspiracies that fueled the insurrectionists' vicious anger at the outcome of a free and fair election.

Much of the Texas GOP's post-siege rhetoric depicts the technology and social media companies' moves as the "censorship of conservatives," even though the actions were in response to credible evidence that communications were inciting violence. And legal experts agree that these tech companies are exercising their full legal rights to moderate anything on their platforms. That means some GOP politicians' vows to take legal, congressional and legislative action now put them in the rare position of advocating for something they typically oppose: more regulation of companies operating in a free market.

Beleaguered Texas Attorney General Ken Paxton, a fervent Trump loyalist who attended the rally that preceded the attack on the US Capitol, even issued civil investigative demands last week to five tech and social media firms, including Facebook and Twitter.

"Texas Republicans Are Angry at Big Tech's Reaction to U.S. Capitol Siege. But Few Mention The GOP's Role in Sowing Election Misinformation," by Duncan Agnew and Bryan Mena, *Texas Tribune*, January 21, 2021. Reprinted by permission.

"The seemingly coordinated de-platforming of the President of the United States and several leading voices not only chills free speech, it wholly silences those whose speech and political beliefs do not align with leaders of Big Tech companies," Paxton said in a Jan. 13 news release.

According to US Code, an attorney general can issue a civil investigative demand during a racketeering investigation in order to acquire information or documents relevant to that investigation. These demands can be used to obtain evidence of a company's procedures and policies. According to last week's press release, Paxton is using civil investigative demands to learn about the procedures that social media firms use to regulate postings or user accounts.

"The public deserves the truth about how these companies moderate and possibly eliminate speech they disagree with," Paxton said.

Following the violent riot at the Capitol, Paxton claimed on Twitter that the mob consisted of "antifa thugs" rather than Trump supporters. FBI assistant director Steven D'Antuono refuted that claim during a news conference, saying that the agency has "no indication" that antifa had anything to do with the violence.

After filing a long shot lawsuit seeking to overturn the election results (which the US Supreme Court quickly rejected), the Texas attorney general has continued to peddle baseless claims of election fraud. He has not acknowledged any personal role in sowing doubts over the election results among far-right fringe groups. Instead, he has used recent days to launch an attack on social media companies.

Trump repeatedly advertised the "Save America" rally for Jan. 6, the day Congress was slated to formally certify the election results, on his Twitter account. He also attacked the results of the election—despite his own Justice Department's finding that there was no evidence of widespread fraud that would have changed the outcome—during his speech to the crowd that day.

"If you don't fight like hell, we're not going to have a country anymore," he told his supporters, just before many of them broke into the Capitol.

Facebook, Twitter and other tech corporations have faced criticism in the past for allowing their platforms to be used to sow misinformation and propagate violence, mostly from Democrats. Democratic lawmakers last year got little traction with a bill in Congress that would have held social media companies accountable for the "amplification of harmful, radicalizing content that leads to offline violence."

The tech companies most recently explained their removal of Trump's accounts in his final days in office by citing concerns that his false claims of election fraud may possibly incite more violence. Other accounts and hashtags like #StopTheSteal that glorified violence or promoted QAnon conspiracies have also been purged by various sites.

"We faced an extraordinary and untenable circumstance, forcing us to focus all of our actions on public safety," Twitter CEO Jack Dorsey said of the platform's decision to ban Trump. "Offline harm as a result of online speech is demonstrably real, and what drives our policy and enforcement above all."

The Washington Post reported that since Twitter and other social media platforms suspended the president's accounts, online misinformation about election fraud has dropped 73%, according to San Francisco-based research firm Zignal Labs. Social media mentions about voter fraud plummeted from 2.5 million to just 688,000 in the week after Trump's removal from Twitter.

## Parler, Paxton and Freedom of Speech

Meanwhile, Apple, Amazon Web Services and other companies also severed ties with the app Parler due to its role in failing to address right-wing conspiracy theories and calls for pro-Tump violence on its platform. The app and website served as a social media forum for groups of far-right extremists and QAnon conspiracy theorists.

After the Capitol siege, ProPublica recreated the scene by aggregating thousands of videos uploaded to Parler showing the pro-Trump mob breaching the walls of the Capitol. On Tuesday, CNN reported that Parler was partially back online with the help of a Russian-based tech company. However, the platform remains mostly unavailable for its millions of users.

On Thursday, the Democratic chairwoman of the House Committee on Oversight and Reform requested that the FBI launch a "robust examination" of Parler's role in the Capitol siege and the site's apparent ties to a Russian firm.

Despite the recent violence at the Capitol and an accompanying string of arrests, Texas Republicans have continued to focus on the threat they believe "big tech" poses to freedom of speech.

In a Jan. 9 statement, Republican Lt. Gov. Dan Patrick condemned the violent siege of the US Capitol by Trump supporters and took a swipe at tech companies, but stopped short of implicating Trump himself in the attack. Patrick chaired Trump's reelection campaign in Texas.

"Enough of allowing Big Tech—Twitter, Google, Facebook and Apple—to silence our freedom of speech," Lt. Gov. Dan Patrick wrote in a Jan. 9 news release. "We cannot let this happen. It will lead to more anger. And enough of all the hate on social media toward those who have a different opinion than we do."

Legal experts, meanwhile, point out that the First Amendment—which protects free speech—only prohibits government censorship. That leaves private companies to choose their own protocols.

"From a First Amendment perspective, social media companies are private actors and aren't subject to the First Amendment," said Scot Powe, a professor at the University of Texas School of Law. "So it's a matter of constitutional law. They can be as biased as they want in any direction they choose."

Still, many Republicans, like freshman US Rep. Beth Van Duyne of Irving, echoed Patrick's sentiments.

"Big Tech is increasingly wielding their power and market dominance to silence conservative voices, and we need to put an end to it," Van Duyne said on Twitter.

Van Duyne was one of 17 Texas Republicans in Congress who voted to contest the electoral votes from at least one of the states Trump lost in November. She decried the violent insurrection at the Capitol in a Jan. 6 Twitter thread, "imploring President Trump to send a clear message by denouncing this sickening violence."

Van Duyne added on Twitter that she is pledging to refuse future campaign contributions from major tech firms. According to campaign finance reports, she did not receive any campaign donations from major tech corporations during the 2020 election cycle.

"Please join me in sending a clear message to those in Silicon Valley: If you're going to censor conservative voices, we don't want your money," Van Duyne said in a Jan. 15 news release.

## A Long Standing Legal Battle

Many Republicans' ire after the Capitol siege has been aimed at a part of the 1996 Communications Decency Act that establishes tech companies as private platforms instead of publishers.

That decades-old law reaffirms the ability of private firms to regulate content as they see fit. And Section 230 of the act protects media companies from legal liability for what their users post. Many Texas Republicans were eyeing a repeal of the section even before the Capitol siege, the cancellation of a sitting president's social media accounts and Trump's second impeachment.

"Section 230 gives every company the freedom to do what it wants," Stanford Law School professor Mark Lemley told the Tribune. "It can moderate or not. And it can decide what to moderate in ways that favor some speech over others. Facebook bans nudity, for instance; other sites don't."

But since Twitter banned Trump, Texans in the GOP have taken to social media to renew their criticisms of Section 230.

US Rep. Lance Gooden, R-Terrell, wrote in a Jan. 7 tweet that Section 230 has allowed "Big Tech to SILENCE the leader of the free world."

But experts say the basic legal rights of private media corporations allow them to remove content or user accounts, and Section 230 only goes an extra step to protect such companies from lawsuits over what their users post.

Gooden objected to Congress' certification of some of the Electoral College votes that gave President Joe Biden the victory over former President Trump. Following the Capitol riot, Gooden condemned the violence on Twitter, but he has continued to back Trump's false claims of election fraud while opposing Biden's "radical agenda."

Gooden's staff did not respond to a request for comment from the Tribune.

## The Fight in the Texas Legislature

Texas Republicans back home have also promised legislation aimed at major tech companies since social media giants and other big firms purged Trump, conspiracy theorists and Parler.

State Rep. Briscoe Cain, R-Deer Park, wants to file legislation completely banning government contracts with companies like Apple, which stopped offering Parler on its app store.

"I've asked my staff to start drafting legislation to prohibit the use of tax dollars to purchase @Apple products," Cain tweeted last week—from an Apple iPhone, according to the tweet. "I hope legislators in other states will do the same."

In a statement to the Tribune, Cain said he enjoys using Twitter and Facebook, but he believes that such companies "unfairly target conservatives" and should not benefit by receiving any tax dollars through government contracts. While using his social media accounts to promote this legislation over the last week, Cain has not condemned the Capitol riot in any of his postings.

Cain's staff did not provide any further information about the details of Texas government contracts with Apple, including

*Big Tech and Democracy*

how much money the state's many independent agencies may pay the company.

State Sen. Carol Alvarado, a Houston Democrat, said such a law banning tech contracts with the government would only disrupt the operations of the state government and create unnecessary difficulties with technology. She added that proposing the kind of law that Cain envisions would distract from the real problems that Texans are facing every day.

"I don't see that people are demanding that we do something about this," Alvarado said. "People want us to fight the virus and to get our economy going again. I hope that people from both sides would focus on those issues and not a solution that's looking for a problem."

# CHAPTER 3

# Does Technology Feed Extremism or Other Harmful Behaviors?

# Overview: Social Media Has Greatly Enabled Extremist Groups

*J. M. Berger*

*J. M. Berger is an analyst and consultant who writes about extremist activities in the United States and how extremists use social media.*

Tens of thousands of foreign fighters found their way to Afghanistan during the 1980s, without benefit of the Internet. More than 900 Americans found their way to Guyana in the 1970s, to die in the Jonestown massacre. Extremists have always found ways to make contact with like-minded recruits.

As new companies sprouted up in the late 1990s and early 2000s, each promised its technology would change everything. They came and they went, some faster than others, some still lingering in a vegetative state. Compuserve, AIM, Napster, Friendster, Tripod, Geocities, MySpace, Digg, and so on. It was hard to take their grandiose claims seriously.

But some survived, including Twitter, Facebook, YouTube, and Reddit, and they changed the global game.

Many of these changes are either neutral or good—from enabling global commerce to empowering free expression in authoritarian societies. But social media has also revolutionized the business of violent extremism perhaps more profoundly than any other sphere.

In 2011, I wrote that terrorists use the Internet the same way that everyone else does. That is no longer true, and perhaps I should have seen it coming sooner.

The last eight months have seen wall-to-wall chaos, with violence coming from multiple directions and diverse ideologies, capable of landing anywhere in the world, attacks that specifically target people by race, religion, gender, and sexual orientation—resulting in widespread fear and anger among people of every identity group. The list goes on

"The Toxic Mix of Extremism and Social Media," by J.M. Berger, PBS, September 7, 2016. Reprinted by permission.

and on and on. Paris, Normandy, Nice, Brussels, Munich, Ansbach, Dhaka, Würzburg, San Bernardino, Orlando, Malheur, Dallas, Baton Rouge, a wave of stabbing attacks in Israel, attacks on mosques and Muslims.

There have been many cosmetic changes to extremist recruitment and radicalization in the Internet era, but also a few fundamental shifts. Recruiting in cyberspace offers critical advantages over meatspace—a term coined from cyberpunk novels of the 1980s and 1990s to describe the old-fashioned world of human bodies in proximity to one another.

One is security. Recruiters can search online for prospects without exposing themselves to scrutiny, and they enjoy better anonymity when they approach a target. Potential recruits can forge relationships with violent extremists before exposing themselves to physical risk in a face-to-face meeting.

Another is discovery. Recruiters and potential recruits can now hunt through a target audience of millions to find each other. Before they were constrained by the cost of travel and the risk of exposure, and the reduced reach that comes with working in meatspace.

Third, recruitment is ultimately about relationships, and in a world of networked social media, it is easier to build intimate relationships over geographic distances, even while maintaining some veneer of anonymity.

Finally, social media rapidly increases the speed of contagion. It took centuries for early Christianity to overwhelm the Roman Empire—enough time for its early apocalyptic strain to evolve and moderate, allowing for the rise of institutions to stabilize its belief system. Today, ideas spread as fast as they change, often faster. For now, at least, the contagion can outrace the evolutionary pressures that push movements into moderation. This shift favors more extreme ideas, which propagate faster than ever before.

## Social Media Successors to ISIS

None of these dynamics are exclusive to jihadism. But all are new developments in social interactions, and all of them have consequences.

The most prolific and extreme offender on social media has been the Islamic State, known as ISIS or ISIL, whose message has been broadcast around the world on social media, with extraordinary speed and success. But the Islamic State's social media effort has peaked, and its successors are already on the rise.

Consider white nationalism, an ideology that went through an extended period of decline, with sharp losses starting in the late 1990s and continuing through the 2000s. The movement's adherents were fragmented, factionalized, and isolated in the face of a powerful social current against overt racism. Now, a mix of political factors and the rise of social networking have sparked a worrying resurgence.

One element of white nationalism's decline was its marginalization from the mainstream of society. The role of mainstream media gatekeepers was crucial in reinforcing that isolation through the second half of the 20th century. Overt white nationalism was rarely found on editorial pages, and its leading figures were rarely seen on the news except in a negative light. Popular entertainment and culture reinforced messages promoting diversity.

Social media was not the only factor driving the return of white nationalism—the election of an African-American president, economic and demographic shifts, and a new flood of refugees from the Syrian civil war all provide important political context. But the mechanics of the resurgence were swifter and more volatile because of instantaneous global networking, and some key offline factors—including the rise of the Islamic State and Donald Trump's racially divisive presidential campaign—have been profoundly empowered by access to social media.

Early social media, such as bulletin boards and message boards, provided rare forums where white nationalists could gather and share their views without fear of censure. But when open social media platforms emerged—including YouTube, Facebook, and Twitter—a pressure valve burst open, releasing a scalding jet of steam.

After decades of being silenced, white nationalists could suddenly organize into significant audiences, sometimes as many as tens of thousands of people, sometimes more. Functional anonymity insulated many adherents from the professional and social consequences of professing overt racism in the real world. And they could project their message to audiences who had not sought them out—hundreds of thousands more.

While estimates of the total population of white nationalist supporters online are less concrete than those for the Islamic State, my preliminary research shows substantial increases in activist social media accounts since 2012, congruent with the rise of nationalist political movements in the United States and Europe. The total, at the least, runs into six figures. (These gains are detailed in my new paper for George Washington University's Program on Extremism.)

## Organized Abuse

None of this comes as a surprise to anyone active on social media. Journalists, experts, celebrities and ordinary people are now routinely exposed to torrents of racist, anti-Semitic, homophobic, and misogynistic abuse. Efforts to highlight this activity and shame the perpetrators often simply encourages the abusers and exposes more people to their message of hate, a paradox familiar to anyone working on jihadist social media.

Much of this abuse is organized rather than spontaneous, and white nationalists are only part of the picture. From "Trumpkins" to "Bernie Bros," antisocial content surrounding contentious online personalities has skyrocketed, carried out by users for whom trolling has become a consuming vocation, in some cases literally.

Online culture has also led to convergence between those who sincerely believe in an extremist ideology, such as Nazism, and those who instrumentalize that ideology as an outlet for less defined antisocial impulses such as harassment and bullying. Some users eventually become true believers after starting out simply as antisocial harassers. Author Jesse Walker called this the "Mother

Night" phenomenon, referring to a Kurt Vonnegut novel whose theme is summed up in the quote: "We are what we pretend to be, so we must be careful about what we pretend to be."

Some pranksters and professional trolls now routinely skip among ideologies, and state-sponsored trolls are often on hand to pour fuel on the fire. One Jewish-American arrested for supporting the Islamic State turned out to be a full-time troll posing as everything from a jihadist to a neo-Nazi to radical feminist. Sometimes he argued with himself using his various accounts. His jihadi persona was virtually indistinguishable from the real thing, and sincere or not, he played a real part in supporting the Islamic State and encouraging terrorist attacks. He will not be the last such chimera we see.

The truly bad news in all of this is that the Islamic State was the easy problem. The hyperactivity and hyperviolence of the Islamic State's social media is prone to break most social media platforms' terms of service, the rules that users agree to when they sign up—that makes it easy for platforms to disable the accounts once they've been identified. The Islamic State is also a discrete organization, an entity with a geographic locus. And it is the ultimate outsider, so incredibly marginalized that virtually no one will advocate on its behalf as its social media accounts are suspended— not even al Qaeda.

Consider, then, the much greater challenge that lies ahead. White nationalism is not an outsider in Western civilization by any reasonable measure. We are scant decades past its overt domination of Western politics, and it is enjoying a resurgence today in the form of nationalist political parties and candidates throughout the Western world. While some white nationalist adherents are careless about the terms of service, many color within the lines, if only barely. While many people are repulsed by white nationalists and their principles, others are busy electing them to public office.

## A Grim Future

The blurred lines create new challenges. Even with Islamic State social networks, a handful of people have objected to disruption and suppression on the basis of free speech concerns while not defending the group itself. For extremist movements that are less brazen and more integrated into host societies, the difficulties multiply.

For instance, sovereign citizen propaganda almost certainly leads some adherents to violence, but the content does not typically cross the line with explicit calls to violence, as defined by most social media companies' terms of service. Race hate without a threat of violence is not consistently suspended despite pertinent rules in social media platforms' terms of service.

These problems cannot be easily solved. There is no central authority to litigate social media conflicts, which cross lines between private companies and public discourse and must accommodate multiple jurisdictions around the globe. Few would favor such an approach even if the many practical obstacles could be surmounted.

Mubin Shaikh went from young army cadet to self-radicalized Jihadist and back. Here's what he learned.

It is possible that some sort of social or technological solution to these challenges will evolve organically, whether through the restructuring of online social platforms, the emergence of truly positive viral movements with real staying power (as opposed to the current paradigm of surge and fade).

But as of now, there is little visible reason for optimism.

While not everyone uses social media, those who do play an increasingly dominant role driving public policy and mainstream media coverage. What happens on social media matters, although it does not always provide a straight line from intention to result.

And although social media is a key facilitator of extremist sprawl, there is also a spillover effect. Public spectacle violence such as ISIS-broadcast decapitations dominates the mainstream media, which takes cues about what to cover from social media, resulting in more coverage that reaches more people, inspiring copycats and creating more curiosity about extremist groups, which can then be satisfied online.

I believe we are seeing the start of a massive social reorganization with serious implications for global and national security.

Salafists and white nationalists already excel at creating online echo chambers, flocking to follow social media accounts focused on grievances related to Muslim prisoners and black violence, respectively. Both white nationalists and jihadists have been hobbled by the lone-wolf model for years, but the rise of super-empowered super-minorities—such as the Islamic State—has created a new path toward the successful mobilization of fractional percentages of global demographic groups.

Russia, Iran, Syria, and other state actors have carefully and strategically built their own echo chambers. Anarchists, socialists, sovereign citizens, and black nationalists are not far behind, although various factors have slowed the crystallization of their social networks.

While there is no consistent estimate of the Islamic State's foreign fighter base, no one believes it is greater than tens of thousands of fighters. Yet combined with its other assets, the Islamic State has thrown the world into a frenzy of activity, both productive and counterproductive.

Ten thousand people are a drop in the bucket compared to the population of the world or even most nations. But 10,000 people acting in concert can disrupt events on a global scale.

One million people comprise less than 0.002% of the world's population. But 1 million people acting in concert can wreak unimaginable havoc. We are marching toward an event of that magnitude, whether next year or in ten years.

We are not ready.

# Extremists Maximize Online Resources

*Megan Squire*

*Megan Squire is a professor of computer science at Elon University in North Carolina. She specializes in understanding extremist online communities.*

W hy is it still so easy to find violent white supremacist content online, even though social media companies keep claiming that they are working overtime to delete it? Last weekend, the El Paso shooter—just like the San Diego and Christchurch shooters back in April—posted his manifesto to the same extremist website and claimed to take inspiration from what he had read there. Mainstream social media companies say they are trying to stop the spread of this kind of violent content, but today's domestic terrorists are highly motivated to stay online, and they are using every trick in the book to stay that way. Fighting a motivated, evolving adversary is a classic challenge of cybersecurity, but the difference here is that lives—not dollars or passwords—hang in the balance.

## Platforms Are Ripe for Abuse

"We need to strike hard, and strike fast. We need complete elimination of the enemy." On July 24, three neo-Nazi podcasters introduced their latest show without mincing words. Men of the white race, they said, should adopt an accelerationist and exterminationist mindset, openly embracing violence against people of color, Jews, LGBT people. "We're going to need our soldiers in the field, not only murdering our enemies…and also being killed in return. There's going to be martyrs."

After 81 minutes, the hosts concluded their show, and this video, like all the other videos produced by this streaming network,

"How Big Tech and Policymakers Miss the Mark When Fighting Online Extremism," by Megan Squire, The Brookings Institution, August 7, 2019. Reprinted by permission.

was immediately removed from YouTube—by its own hosts. They know it is far too risky to leave the video up on their channel. YouTube's guidelines prohibit violent speech, and because of its three strikes policy, if enough people flag the video, the entire channel could be banned. Plus, the hosts know they really only need YouTube for its interactive chats and high bandwidth during the livestream itself. So why take the risk of leaving the show on YouTube?

Instead, the hosts relocated the video to Bitchute, a small, UK-based peer-to-peer video hosting service with looser rules governing acceptable content. As of this writing, the video was flagged but has not been removed from Bitchute. Since then, the podcasters have uploaded four additional videos this same way, one of which lauded the "body count" of the El Paso terror attack ("20 dead, 26 wounded? Fantastic, fantastic.") before reading the manifesto in its entirety and providing commentary.

I relate this story because it is a canary in the coal mine for future battles over content moderation. "Big Tech" continues to promise increasingly complex AI-based moderation schemes, while exhibiting willful blindness about the simple ways in which their services are being abused. These podcasters are just one example of persistent, motivated threat actors intentionally probing the limitations of content moderation to see what they can get away with, and modifying their behavior accordingly. YouTube, owned by a company with an $800 billion market cap, seems unable or unwilling to acknowledge that their content moderation has been trampled for over a year by three guys with a microphone and a couple of extra Gmail accounts. After the Christchurch attack, Facebook announced new video streaming rules that are similarly reactive, designed to stop the last mass shooter, not to anticipate what the next one will do.

## Focused on Yesterday's Problems

Now, critics of Big Tech are lining up to plead, cajole, and threaten—from the left and right. In June, Senators Cruz (R-TX) and Hawley (R-

MO) proposed legislation that would require social media companies over a certain size to prove no political bias when moderating content. Convinced that conservatives voices are being unfairly targeted, they followed up with a letter to the Federal Trade Commission asking for an investigation into moderation policies on Facebook, YouTube, and Twitter. In July, Tulsi Gabbard (D-HI), candidate for the Democratic nomination for President, filed suit against Google for, among other things, "playing favorites, with no warning, no transparency—and no accountability" in their content moderation.

As with the reactive policies implemented by the media companies themselves, this legislation and lawsuit are also naïvely focused on yesterday's problems. They do not acknowledge the way the platforms are actually being gamed today, nor how they will be abused tomorrow.

Serial harassers and trolls will always figure out tricks to avoid the bans, and even if they somehow catch a block that sticks, the growing "Alt Tech" ecosystem made of decentralized, niche services often located in other countries, is more than willing to scoop them up. Finally banned from YouTube? Try Bitchute or DLive. De-platformed from Facebook or Twitter? Try Telegram, Parler, or Gab—the site favored by the Pittsburgh synagogue shooter back in October 2018—or the so-called "image boards" like 8chan, where the Christchurch, San Diego, and El Paso shooters all posted their manifestos.

There are dozens of these barely-moderated havens for extremism online right now, and none of them will be affected by legislation proposed to supposedly rid US-based Big Tech of hatred. In fact, most of these sites do not bother to conduct any meaningful self-regulation and are too small to qualify for monitoring under proposed legislation. Making things worse, when a "Big Tech" site is removed, an "Alt-Tech" clone rises up to take its place. Thus, the real danger slips right through the cracks.

## Expand Your Expertise

And so, we are at an impasse. Legislative and corporate policies are designed to solve a specific problem for a particular stakeholder at a set time and place. In contrast, the online hate ecosystem is volatile, unpredictable, constantly changing, and deliberately confusing. Battling hate and extremism online has much in common with the attack-and-defend world of cybersecurity in which the attacker only has to successfully exploit one crack in the system, while the defender must guard 100% of it.

So just like with cybersecurity, solving the problem of extremism online will include significant investment in expertise. Social media companies must acknowledge that their current understanding of the groups and individuals that pose the most risk is lacking, at best. While dozens of virulently racist podcasters and video streamers routinely game the system and build their audiences, Big Tech instead issues bans of high-profile clowns and trolls. These companies need to broadly expand their in-house knowledge so they can tackle white supremacist extremism as it really looks online today. If such rapid skill-up is not possible, then they need to call in outside experts with real experience—quickly.

The Alt-Tech clone ecosystem is currently surviving on extremely thin margins and succeeds because of the short attention span of the media. For example, 8chan is in the news currently as it is dropped from mainstream hosting providers, but its software is open source and a copycat site with a slightly different name can be created easily. Alt-Tech companies are also scrambling to provide replacement infrastructure services for sites that have been de-platformed.

But we saw similar attention-boredom cycles in August 2017 following the deadly Unite the Right events in Charlottesville. The Daily Stormer and Stormfront, two notorious neo-Nazi sites, were banned following a high-profile but temporary media outrage cycle. The resilience of Stormfront in particular is troubling as it has a very long tenure online and its users have been tied to over 100 murders. Without strong public pressure resulting from consistent, long-term media coverage, these sites easily resurface within days or hours of a ban.

As for policymakers, instead of cutting budgets for extremism prevention, why not expand them? Instead of creating distracting side shows and political theater that belie any real understanding of violent extremism and how it spreads, focus on hammering out long-term strategies to tackle an increasingly decentralized, encrypted internet and a rapidly expanding Alt-Tech ecosystem.

It will be impossible to make real headway in combating the spread of violent extremism online without a realistic understanding of how internet platforms are being abused today, and an admission from the social media companies and policymakers that they do not really understand the phenomenon. Expertise and transparency remain critical to combating the spread of hate online. Otherwise, extremists will continue to stay one step ahead, using technology to fundraise, recruit, and radicalize with impunity.

# Social Media Affects Mental Health

*McLean Hospital*

*McLean Hospital is an affiliate of Harvard Medical School and specializes in mental health.*

The social media platform Instagram made headlines last year for suppressing likes in an effort to curb the comparisons and hurt feelings associated with attaching popularity to sharing content. But do these efforts combat mental health issues, or are they simply applying a band-aid to a wound?

It's a small step in the right direction, says Jacqueline Sperling, PhD, a psychologist at McLean Hospital who works with youth who experience anxiety disorders, about Instagram's recent restriction. "Even if you remove the likes, there continue to be opportunities for comparisons and feedback. People still can compare themselves to others, and people still can post comments."

## The Risks for the Reward

Social media has a reinforcing nature. Using it activates the brain's reward center by releasing dopamine, a "feel-good chemical" linked to pleasurable activities such as sex, food, and social interaction. The platforms are designed to be addictive and are associated with anxiety, depression, and even physical ailments.

According to the Pew Research Center, 69% of adults and 81% of teens in the U.S. use social media. This puts a large amount of the population at an increased risk of feeling anxious, depressed, or ill over their social media use.

But what makes users come back for more even when it can literally make them feel sick?

"When the outcome is unpredictable, the behavior is more likely to repeat," Sperling says. "Think of a slot machine: if game players

"The Social Dilemma: Social Media and Your Mental Health," McLean Hospital, February 9, 2021. Reprinted by permission.

knew they never were going to get money by playing the game, then they never would play. The idea of a potential future reward keeps the machines in use. The same goes for social media sites. One does not know how many likes a picture will get, who will 'like' the picture, and when the picture will receive likes. The unknown outcome and the possibility of a desired outcome can keep users engaged with the sites."

To boost self-esteem and feel a sense of belonging in their social circles, people post content with the hope of receiving positive feedback. Couple that content with the structure of potential future reward, and you get a recipe for constantly checking platforms.

When reviewing others' social activity, people tend to make comparisons such as, "Did I get as many likes as someone else?," or "Why didn't this person like my post, but this other person did?" They're searching for validation on the internet that serves as a replacement for meaningful connection they might otherwise make in real life.

FOMO—fear of missing out—also plays a role. If everyone else is using social media sites, and if someone doesn't join in, there's concern that they'll miss jokes, connections, or invitations. Missing experiences can create anxiety and depression. When people look online and see they're excluded from an activity, it can affect thoughts and feelings, and can affect them physically.

A 2018 British study tied social media use to decreased, disrupted, and delayed sleep, which is associated with depression, memory loss, and poor academic performance. Social media use can affect users' physical health even more directly. Researchers know the connection between the mind and the gut can turn anxiety and depression into nausea, headaches, muscle tension, and tremors.

## The Digital Age of Vulnerability

The earlier teens start using social media, the greater impact the platforms have on mental health. This is especially true for females. While teen males tend to express aggression physically, females do so relationally by excluding others and sharing hurtful comments. Social media increases the opportunity for such harmful interactions.

Sperling offers the example of a seventh grader whose best friend chooses a new best friend and posts pictures of the pair at the movies or on a weekend trip. "Twenty years ago, the girl may have been excluded from her best friend's activities, but she may not have known about it unless she was told explicitly," Sperling says.

In addition to providing young people with a window through which they can view missed experiences, social media puts a distorted lens on appearances and reality. Facebook, Instagram, and Snapchat increase the likelihood of seeing unrealistic, filtered photos at a time when teen bodies are changing.

In the past, teens read magazines that contained altered photos of models. Now, these images are one thumb-scroll away at any given time. Apps that provide the user with airbrushing, teeth whitening, and more filters are easy to find and easier to use. It's not only celebrities who look perfect—it's everyone.

When there's a filter applied to the digital world, it can be hard for teens to tell what's real and what isn't, which comes at a difficult time for them physically and emotionally.

"Middle school already is challenging for students with all of their developmental changes. As they go through puberty, they're tasked with establishing their identity at a time when the frontal lobes in their brains are not fully developed, and there is a lack of impulse control. All of this happens while their relationships with peers become more important," Sperling says. "It's a very vulnerable population to have access to something where there is no stopgap before they post or press the send button. I think that's something of which to be mindful."

Adults are vulnerable, too. In recent years, plastic surgeons have seen an uptick in requests from patients who want to look like their filtered Snapchat and Instagram photos. A *New York Times* article that ran in June 2018 features a newlywed couple who nearly separated after their honeymoon. The reason: the wife spent more time on the trip planning and posting selfies than she spent with her husband.

## How Can the Platforms Change?

Sperling acknowledges social platforms have positive aspects, such as their ability to allow people to stay in touch with family and friends around the world. She realizes the potential pitfalls of completely banning teens from sites that have become a part of life for their generation—not just as a way for them to stay on top of recent parties and conversations but often as an expected source of announcements and news. Still, she says, the platforms have opened a "Pandora's box" as they continue to evolve more quickly than we can research their impact.

"I think we need to take a step back and look at the role technology is playing in our society as a whole, in terms of people needing instant gratification, staying home and not interacting in the community by going to local stores or to the movie theater," she says. "Even dating apps can decrease motivation for single adults to approach others in the community if they think they just can connect with them on an app first."

In addition to limiting likes, as Instagram has done, Sperling suggests social platforms consider decreasing mass sharing altogether. They might function more as messaging services by highlighting one-on-one communications. Regardless of how likely social media giants are to change their ways, though, individuals can take control of their own behavior.

## Distract Yourself from the Distraction

People aren't usually motivated to change their social media use by simply hearing it's bad for them. It's better for individuals to see what their limits are. It's probably unrealistic for most social media users to quit completely. However, they can monitor their behavior to see how their use impacts them, and how to act as a result.

Michelle knows this all too well. When she was initially treated for anxiety, her therapist asked her if she was active on social media, and she said yes. "It turns out that a lot of my anxiety and impostor syndrome is made worse when I'm online." A person experiences impostor syndrome when feeling chronic self-doubt and a sense of being exposed as 'a fraud' in terms of success and intellect. "Whether it's another pretty vacation or someone's bouquet of flowers, my mind went from 'Why not me?' to 'I don't deserve those things, and I don't know why,' and it made me feel awful."

She and her therapist decided to set ground rules. "If I was to continue using social media, I had to learn what would trigger my anxiety and how using different platforms made me feel," says Michelle. The result was her deleting Snapchat for good, and after 5 years, she still doesn't miss it. She's still active on several other platforms, though.

Sperling encourages people to conduct their own behavior experiments by rating their emotions on a scale of 0-10, with 10 being the most intensely one could experience an emotion, before and after using social media sites at the same time each day for a week. If one notices that one feels less happy after using them, then one might consider changing how one uses social media sites, such as using them for less time and doing other activities that one enjoys instead.

A 2018 University of Pennsylvania study suggests that such self-monitoring can change one's perception of social media.

The study's researchers looked at 143 undergraduates randomly assigned to two groups. The first set was asked to limit Facebook, Instagram, and Snapchat to ten minutes per platform per day, while the second was asked to continue to use their social media as usual for three weeks. The limited group showed significant reductions in loneliness and depression during those three weeks over the group that continued using social media.

Both groups showed significant decreases in anxiety and fear of missing out compared to where they were at the study's beginning.

"I'd love to say that my use is totally healthy, but I find that I'm still comparing myself to others," Michelle says. "Now I can recognize what's going to help or hurt my mental well-being. My therapist and I agreed that I'd set limits on my app usage to two hours a day across all platforms. Now I know when it's time to log off and take care of myself."

## Set a Good Example

Parents can develop a plan of how much time family members will spend on devices. Strategies like these teach kids healthy media use and good sleep hygiene.

When teens start using social media, parents can ask them to turn in their phones at night with the understanding that parents can review posts and messages. This helps parents be in the know, as sometimes young people will share struggles online while parents have no idea.

Monitoring also encourages teens to remember that everything they share online is a permanent fingerprint. If they don't want their parents to see it, then it shouldn't be posted.

Sperling suggests that some families modify the ways they use social media. Try a "no selfie" policy or a rule that kids can post pictures of tangible objects but no photos of themselves. This way, children can share their experiences without emphasizing a focus on their appearance.

A common argument is when children say they are missing out because of restrictions placed on their phone use—that they aren't allowed on a platform or can't be online after a certain time.

Sperling tells parents to remind kids that a good friend would find a way to spend time with them. She suggests other ways for kids to talk to one another to keep those feelings of FOMO away and be socially present. "If adolescents know that they cannot use their phone after a certain time or are not allowed to access a site that their friends use, then they can ask their friends to let them know of any plans made when they see each other at school or call the house phone or one of the parent's phones so that they can remain included."

Of course, Sperling says, the way parents are using social media is the model for their kids. A University of Texas review of research on parents' use of mobile devices while interacting with their children found that mobile use contributed to distracted parenting, an increase of bids for attention when the parents were distracted, and conflicts with other caregivers.

"Parents' frequency of electronics use can set the tone for what is permissible to their children," Sperling says. "If you want your children to put their phones down at dinner, that will be more likely to happen if you do the same."

# Free Speech Issues Should Be Decided by Users

*Jillian C. York*

*Jillian C. York is the director for international freedom of expression at the Electronic Frontier Foundation.*

On January 7, following the violent white supremacist riots that breached the US Capitol, Twitter and Facebook both suspended President Donald Trump from their platforms. The next day, Twitter made its suspension permanent. Many praised the decision for preventing the president from doing more harm at a time when his adherents are taking cues from his false claims that the election was rigged. Republicans criticized it as a violation of Trump's free speech.

It wasn't. Just as Trump has the First Amendment right to spew deranged nonsense, so too do tech companies have the First Amendment right to remove that content. While some pundits have called the decision unprecedented—or "a turning point for the battle for control over digital speech," as Edward Snowden tweeted—it's not: not at all. Not only do Twitter and Facebook regularly remove all types of protected expression, but Trump's case isn't even the first time the platforms have removed a major political figure.

Following reports of genocide in Myanmar, Facebook banned the country's top general and other military leaders who were using the platform to foment hate. The company also bans Hezbollah from its platform because of its status as a US-designated foreign terror organization, despite the fact that the party holds seats in Lebanon's parliament. And it bans leaders in countries under US sanctions.

At the same time, both Facebook and Twitter have stuck to the tenet that content posted by elected officials deserves more protection than material from ordinary individuals, thus giving politicians' speech more power than that of the people. This position is at odds with plenty of evidence that hateful speech from public figures has a greater impact than similar speech from ordinary users.

Clearly, though, these policies aren't applied evenly around the world. After all, Trump is far from the only world leader using these platforms to foment unrest. One need only look to the BJP, the party of India's Prime Minister Narendra Modi, for more examples.

Though there are certainly short-term benefits—and plenty of satisfaction—to be had from banning Trump, the decision (and those that came before it) raise more foundational questions about speech. Who should have the right to decide what we can and can't say? What does it mean when a corporation can censor a government official?

Facebook's policy staff, and Mark Zuckerberg in particular, have for years shown themselves to be poor judges of what is or isn't appropriate expression. From the platform's ban on breasts to its tendency to suspend users for speaking back against hate speech, or its total failure to remove calls for violence in Myanmar, India, and elsewhere, there's simply no reason to trust Zuckerberg and other tech leaders to get these big decisions right.

## Repealing 230 Isn't the Answer

To remedy these concerns, some are calling for more regulation. In recent months, demands have abounded from both sides of the aisle to repeal or amend Section 230—the law that protects companies from liability for the decisions they make about the content they host—despite some serious misrepresentations from politicians who should know better about how the law actually works.

The thing is, repealing Section 230 would probably not have forced Facebook or Twitter to remove Trump's tweets, nor would it prevent companies from removing content they find disagreeable, whether that content is pornography or the unhinged rantings of

Trump. It is companies' First Amendment rights that enable them to curate their platforms as they see fit.

Instead, repealing Section 230 would hinder competitors to Facebook and the other tech giants, and place a greater risk of liability on platforms for what they choose to host. For instance, without Section 230, Facebook's lawyers could decide that hosting anti-fascist content is too risky in light of the Trump administration's attacks on antifa.

This is not a far-fetched scenario: Platforms already restrict most content that could be even loosely connected to foreign terrorist organizations, for fear that material-support statutes could make them liable. Evidence of war crimes in Syria and vital counter-speech against terrorist organizations abroad have been removed as a result. Similarly, platforms have come under fire for blocking any content seemingly connected to countries under US sanctions. In one particularly absurd example, Etsy banned a handmade doll, made in America, because the listing contained the word "Persian."

It's not difficult to see how ratcheting up platform liability could cause even more vital speech to be removed by corporations whose sole interest is not in "connecting the world" but in profiting from it.

## Platforms Needn't Be Neutral, but They Must Play Fair

Despite what Senator Ted Cruz keeps repeating, there is nothing requiring these platforms to be neutral, nor should there be. If Facebook wants to boot Trump—or photos of breastfeeding mothers—that's the company's prerogative. The problem is not that Facebook has the right to do so, but that—owing to its acquisitions and unhindered growth—its users have virtually nowhere else to go and are stuck dealing with increasingly problematic rules and automated content moderation.

The answer is not repealing Section 230 (which again, would hinder competition) but in creating the conditions for more competition. This is where the Biden administration should focus its attention in the coming months. And those efforts must include reaching out to content moderation experts from advocacy and academia to understand the range of problems faced by users worldwide, rather than simply focusing on the debate inside the US.

As for platforms, they know what they need to do, because civil society has told them for years. They must be more transparent and ensure that users have the right to remedy when wrong decisions are made. The Santa Clara Principles on Transparency and Accountability in Content Moderation—endorsed in 2019 by most major platforms but adhered to by only one (Reddit)—offer minimum standards for companies on these measures. Platforms should also stick to their existing commitments to responsible decision-making. Most important, they should ensure that the decisions they make about speech are in line with global human rights standards, rather than making the rules up as they go.

Reasonable people can disagree on whether the act of banning Trump from these platforms was the right one, but if we want to ensure that platforms make better decisions in the future, we mustn't look to quick fixes.

# Individual Human Action Can Maximize the Benefits of Technology

*Kerry McDonald*

*Kerry McDonald is a senior education fellow at FEE and author of* Unschooled: Raising Curious, Well-Educated Children Outside the Conventional Classroom *(Chicago Review Press, 2019). She is also an adjunct scholar at the Cato Institute and a regular* Forbes *contributor.*

I watched *The Social Dilemma* with my 12-year-old son this week and it couldn't be more timely.

A Netflix original docu-drama that was released last fall, The Social Dilemma emphasizes how the underlying algorithms and business models of social media companies keep us hooked and could contribute to polarization.

Most of the film features former social media executives and programmers who describe how features as benign as the social media "Like" button, intended to spread goodwill, may have the opposite effect. When we don't get enough "Likes" we can feel deflated. This may be particularly true of teenagers and pre-teens, who have experienced increasing rates of anxiety and depression in recent years, although research suggests this trend has little to do with social media usage.

There is an anti-capitalism sentiment that also pervades the film (profits over people!) and appears alongside some moral panic about how technology could destroy us all. Throughout the documentary, it becomes more clear that the filmmakers believe government regulation of social media and Big Tech is the answer. Indeed, this is something that both major political parties support, and it is gaining new momentum in 2021.

But is government regulation really the answer?

"Families, Not the Government, Should Regulate Big Tech," by Kerry McDonald, Foundation for Economic Education, January 15, 2021, https://fee.org/articles/families-not-the-government-should-regulate-big-tech/. Licensed under CC BY-4.0 International.

## Riots, Bans, and Moral Panic

It was particularly interesting to watch *The Social Dilemma* after the recent attack on the Capitol, a horrific act of violence following peaceful protests. As FEE's Jon Miltimore and Brad Polumbo eloquently wrote last week: "Political protest loses moral and constitutional legitimacy as soon as it becomes destructive or violent. All Americans have the right to speak out and make our case in the public square. But the moment the first brick is thrown or a window is smashed, it crosses the line between exercising rights and violating the rights of others."

It has been widely claimed that social media, and particularly the small conservative Twitter competitor Parler, are to blame for the Capitol riot, despite well-regarded journalists such as Glenn Greenwald reporting that it was actually on Facebook and YouTube where most of the incitement took place. A Parler executive told Greenwald that none of the people arrested for the breach of the Capitol appeared to be active users of the platform. Parler, nevertheless, was stripped of its Amazon cloud-computing services and removed from both the Apple and Google app stores, causing the platform to be at least temporarily inaccessible. Meanwhile, President Trump's Twitter account has been permanently suspended, and he has been blocked from using his other social media accounts. Other voices have been similarly purged.

Even Ron Paul, the longtime libertarian advocate of peace and non-violence, saw his Facebook page temporarily suspended, a move that Facebook representatives later said was a mistake.

Watching *The Social Dilemma*, it's easy to think that social media and Big Tech have caused our social strife and must be urgently regulated by government officials, who can allegedly make them kinder and gentler. The film makes it seem that this is a moral imperative, lest we destroy ourselves and our civilization. Historically, new technologies have caused similar fears about our demise.

"We shall soon be nothing but transparent heaps of jelly to each other," a writer once lamented about a new technology that was overtaking society and causing widespread concern and disruption. What was this high-tech curse?

The telephone.

## What Can We Do As Individuals and Families?

This is not to say that we shouldn't be concerned about the ways social media and technology could influence our lives and our perceptions, and particularly the minds of our children and teens. The film does a good job of illustrating how artificial intelligence and social media algorithms keep us engaged, and in some cases perhaps even addicted, to checking our smartphones and browsing our Instagram feeds. Understanding the subtle ways in which these technologies and platforms work is important so that we can choose our actions more wisely.

Individual human action, not government regulation, can help us maximize the benefits of technology and social media while minimizing their drawbacks.

"Human action is purposeful behavior," economist Ludwig von Mises wrote in *Human Action: A Treatise on Economics*. "Or we may say: Action is will put into operation and transformed into an agency, is aiming at ends and goals, is the ego's meaningful response to stimuli and to the conditions of its environment, is a person's conscious adjustment to the state of the universe that determines his life."

Here are five ideas for turning action into agency regarding Big Tech and social media:

### 1. Understand the Algorithms

Recognize how social media algorithms work to keep us on these platforms and to select what we see and don't see, and talk about these processes with our kids. Understanding how we are being influenced can help us take more control of our social media usage.

### 2. Be Discerning

As consumers, we can pick and choose from a variety of different social media platforms and give our time and attention to those we most value. For example, after President Trump was banned from

Twitter, the company's stock price plummeted, as conservative users fled the platform. If we don't like a company's practices, we can leave. Our consumer actions are significant.

### 3. Explore (And Invent!) Alternatives

Despite claims that Big Tech is monopolistic and therefore must be regulated, there are already many alternatives. TechCrunch reported this week that social networks such as MeWe and CloutHub are booming. Entrepreneurs continue to invent new social networking products and services that meet changing consumer demand. Government regulation of Big Tech could actually stifle competition. For instance, executives at large social media companies like Facebook are asking to be regulated, setting up roadblocks for smaller companies to enter the market.

### 4. Set Guidelines and Limits

We can establish healthy parameters for our own use of technology and social media, and help our children to do the same. Psychologist and author Jonathan Haidt recommends that parents wait until their children are high school-age before they get access to social media. On the other hand, I find the argument made by psychologist and author Jordan Shapiro more compelling. He suggests that it can be better to introduce technologies to children earlier when parents have more influence over our children and can help them better navigate these tools. Parents are, of course, the ones who know their children best and can decide what technology approach works well for their children and teens.

### 5. Prioritize In-Person Interaction

Lockdowns and pandemic policies have cut us off physically from each other and could contribute to some of the social unrest of the past several months. Prioritizing in-person interactions for ourselves and our children and teens is crucial, whether that is prioritizing family time, eating dinner together, gathering with friends, or taking a walk with neighbors. Researchers have found that during lockdowns nearly half of young adults show signs of depression, and younger children's mental health has deteriorated "substantially." Parents can encourage their children and teens to see friends in person rather than only on screens.

We can take personal action to manage Big Tech and social media concerns through our choices and behaviors. Empowering the government to regulate technology companies and social media will only exacerbate division and unrest. As FEE's Hannah Cox writes: "We now have a gigantic federal government that involves itself in everything from healthcare to education to marriage to social media. This is the root cause of our division."

We should reduce the power of the federal government to regulate our lives, while taking individual action to ensure that the relationship we and our children have with social media and technology is as healthy and productive as possible.

The government doesn't need to protect us. We can protect ourselves, and our children, by better understanding how social media influences us and by taking action as individuals and families. As the journalist H.L. Mencken warned, "The urge to save humanity is almost always only a false-face for the urge to rule it." Self-regulation, not government regulation, is the solution to social media and Big Tech woes.

CHAPTER 4

# Should Technology Be Changed for the Good of Society?

# Overview: Congress Must Play a Critical Role in Solving the Dilemmas Big Tech Presents

## *The Shorenstein Center on Media, Politics and Public Policy*

*The Shorenstein Center on Media, Politics and Public Policy is a Harvard Kennedy School research center dedicated to exploring and illuminating the intersection of press, politics, and public policy in theory and practice.*

Technology has reached a critical juncture in American society. The unfettered optimism of recent decades is now tempered by rising concerns over privacy and security, the impact of disinformation campaigns, and increasing calls for digital accountability. It is clear that the 116th Congress will face pressure to shape technological innovation through policies that protect and serve the best interests of their constituents.

In March 2019, two projects at Harvard Kennedy School—the Technology and Public Purpose (TAPP) Project at the Belfer Center for Science and International Affairs and the Platform Accountability Project at the Shorenstein Center for Media, Politics and Public Policy—hosted a workshop for Congressional staff to identify and discuss policy approaches to the dilemmas of big tech platforms. Rather than seeking consensus or prematurely delving into specific solutions, the day-long educational workshop sought to create an open space for discussion among congressional staffers and experts in the field. Underscoring the interest in this topic, the workshop included Chiefs of Staff, Committee Counsels, and Legislative Directors from both Senate and House offices.

At the outset, Former Secretary of Defense and Belfer Center Director Ash Carter emphasized the responsibility that policymakers

"Big Tech and Democracy: The Critical Role of Congress," by Shorenstein Center on Media, Politics and Public Policy, April 23, 2019. https://shorensteincenter.org/big-tech-democracy-critical-role-congress/. Licensed under CC BY-3.0 Unported.

have in shaping emerging technology. By drawing parallels to other "disruptive tech" from the past, such as nuclear technology, Carter stressed the historic opportunity to shape today's technology for the human good: "Once invented, it can't be undone." Secretary Carter proceeded to lay the groundwork on how case studies from other revolutionary communication technologies, such as the postal service, telegraph, radio, and telephone, can provide insight into the existing toolbox of self-regulation, antitrust, and regulatory solutions.

The opening panel featured several experts who were centrally involved with some of the major reforms in telecommunications and media. The similarities in these historical parallels suggested that today's Congress ought to seek 21st century solutions for 20th century problems. Representing a wide range of expertise regarding antitrust, the private sector, and regulatory agencies, the panel included: Toni Bush, former Senate Commerce Senior Counsel; Mignon Clyburn, former FCC Commissioner; Dipayan Ghosh, Pozen Fellow at the Shorenstein Center and former privacy and public policy advisor at Facebook; Gene Kimmelman, former Chief Counsel of the Justice Department's Antitrust Division; Hong Qu, Program Director for Technology at the Shorenstein Center and former User Interface Designer at YouTube; and Tom Wheeler, former FCC Chairman.

The panelists explored the multitude of issues at play in the big tech space, namely competition, content accountability, privacy and security, accessibility, and protection of civil rights and liberties [See the full event briefing packet for an in-depth discussion of these key issues]. However, the panel expressed concern over issue identification. "It always worries me that we are addressing the symptoms and not the malady," said Clyburn. As part of their discussion, the speakers debated whether market shortcomings related to key issues of democracy could be emanating from the fundamental economics of digital platforms (e.g., network effects, economies of scale and scope) as well as big tech's underlying business model, which centers on user data exploitation. As a result, the panelists agreed that any path toward sustainable policy solutions must first begin through a public and national debate.

Congress has a critical role in setting this agenda by launching a concerted effort of hearings and engaging a diverse set of actors.

During the event, congressional staff were able to further delve into specific questions and concerns regarding tech policy issues through facilitated breakout groups that were joined by expert panelists.

The discussion surfaced four key insights on the tech policy challenges facing Congress and how legislators could more effectively engage with the dilemmas of big tech:

## 1) The Digital Marketplace and New Business Models Are Creating Gaps in Governance Authority and Coordination

The digital marketplace and emerging business models within the tech industry have disrupted the traditional structures of regulation and oversight. While certain issue span across the jurisdictions of Congress or regulatory agencies, others challenges are novel and evidence authority gaps. This has complicated problem identification within an under-resourced Congress.

## 2) A Healthy Mix Between Self-Regulation And Government Policy Is Necessary

There is a variety of corporate and government policy options available to address issues related to big tech and democracy—ranging from self-regulation to antitrust enforcement and regulatory reform. History offers many examples, such as the corporate restructuring of AT&T and the Cable Act of 1992, where similar problems were addressed with vastly different solutions.

## 3) Congressional Hearings Are Underutilized on Technology-Relevant Topics

Congress has a critical role in advancing the public debate on tech policy issues through thematic and granular hearings. In recent years, however, there has been a substantial reduction in the number of Congressional hearings, and the hearings that are held are increasingly used as opportunities for political messaging instead of investigative opportunities to inform policy making. More substantive and frequent hearings can increase policymaker awareness, hold companies accountable to the public interest, and inform the American people.

## 4) Tech Policy Debates Are Still "Pre-Partisan"

The American people, regardless of their political allegiance, are negatively affected by non-competitive markets, privacy breaches, or inequitable access, bias, and discrimination. The current tech policy environment is nascent and it presents a rare opportunity to advance sustainable solutions through a united, bipartisan front.

This is a historic opportunity to guide the Information Age toward a promising future. The educational workshop adds to a vibrant, deliberate, and increasingly growing conversation among congressional leaders and the public to frame big tech policy solutions. Now, our leaders must spark the urgency of this moment in order to protect American consumers, promote innovation and competition as pillars of American enterprise, ensure an informed citizenry, and preserve our democratic values.

## Key Insights

### Gaps in Governance Authority and Coordination

The evolution of technology has not always aligned with the structure of governments. In recent decades, the digital marketplace and technological developments that have caused sectors to appear, disappear, and merge has complicated Congressional legislation and oversight.[1] The emerging business model of today's tech economy has resulted in gaps in governance authority. For instance, the ambiguous identity of platform companies has clashed with the traditional responsibilities of publishers and content providers. In some particular cases, such as tech platform interoperability or data transparency, there is no agency with direct governance authority over the issue.

In Congress, this issue has contributed to a number of overlapping jurisdictions and frustrated coordination efforts where policy questions about a specific technologies are often being considered simultaneously in multiple committees and/or subcommittees. These duplicative efforts further limit Congress' ability to effectively leverage their oversight capacity over Executive branch agencies, where it is often unclear which agency holds the appropriate authority. The combination of these challenges has contributed to an unfocused definition of the problems at hand.

In order to advance the conversation on public good and big tech, it is crucial to clearly and precisely identify the problem that needs to be addressed. As the panelists and participants expressed, this can be difficult due to the wide range of issues, such as content accountability, privacy, security, accessibility, and civil rights and civil liberty protections. Yet as many of the panelists cautioned, these might all be indicators of the larger problem of a business model centered on data. "I think the key is to follow the money," Toni Bush advised. "Fake news, misinformation, etc. are all larger symptoms of the fact that these are advertising platforms and their decision making is driven by revenue." Therefore, the inconvenient truth could be that the incentives of the marketplace are presently misaligned with consumer interests.

The problem identification dilemma is further complicated by Congress' resource constraints. In the past couple of decades, there has been a consistent decline in the number of Congressional staffers in both personal and committee offices. This reduced workforce works on myriad issues and frequently cite a lack of bandwidth and the need to be "a mile wide and an inch deep" as a challenge when trying to engage on new and technical policy issues. This bandwidth challenge is compounded by a lack of constituent focus and/or pressure on science and technology (S&T) issues like big tech platforms. Many staffers note that Congress tends to be reactionary—in large part due to their resource constraints—so without pressure from constituents on S&T issues, it is significantly less likely that proactive policy concerning big tech platforms will be pursued.

Ambiguous jurisdiction, an unfocused definition of the problem, and significant resource constraints have stalled the path to progress.

## A Healthy Mix of Self-Regulation and Government Policy

Leibniz's Law states that no two objects have exactly the same properties. The same principle could be applied to policy prescriptions. Market concentration is not a new phenomenon. The history of U.S. competition law dates back to the late 19th century. Tom Wheeler, former FCC chairman, emphasized this familiar history in his remarks: "We have been here before. We have dealt with these kinds of issues before. The lesson we must take away from these past experiences is that fleeing the challenge is failure. You have to confront it." Congress should indeed confront this history and extract lessons from the many similarities. Yet when addressing today's tech challenges, there is a full range of options varying from self-regulation, to policy guidance, legislative and administrative regulation, and antitrust reform for Congress to explore. Considering a healthy mix of options will ensure that each issue can be addressed with an appropriate solution.

The telephone and cable industries provide two key case studies that demonstrate the outcomes of deploying different policy options to similar problems.

The breakup of the telephone industry manifested in the Department of Justice's antitrust lawsuit against AT&T in 1974. While the case ultimately resulted in the separation of AT&T's long-distance telephone service from regional telephone service, the divestiture case took almost a decade from start to finish. It ended up being a drawn-out and complicated process for a corporate structure, and its accompanying assets, that was comparatively much simpler than the structure of today's big tech companies. In addition, the success of this divestiture is debated as the regional telephone companies, known as Baby Bells, were ultimately reintegrated and long distance competitors folded back into their corporate control. However, the divestiture did introduce greater interoperability in the telephone marketplace that was crucial for technological innovation and future internet competition.

The Cable Act of 1992, on the other hand, represents a regulatory policy solution to promote competition. Similar to the breakup of AT&T, the Cable Act sought to address the vertical integration of cable companies that controlled both the cable service and the content of their channels. By enforcing nondiscrimination in the sale and distribution of content, Congress used the Cable Act to promote diversity in information sources and news. This is analogous in many ways to how several big tech platforms operate as both the marketplace owner and a participant, prioritizing their products and/or content over their competitors.

Accordingly, policymakers can draw many parallels and distinctions between the tools used to address problems that the AT&T breakup and the Cable Act of 1992 were designed to tackle. As Dipayan Ghosh, Pozen Fellow at the Shorenstein Center, noted, "At the highest level there is no difference between AT&T and these contemporary companies, as they are also natural monopolies and vertically integrated." Ghosh went on to say it is worth dissecting how these companies operate and says it is very simple to see how three tenets drive the business model that governs the consumer internet:

1.  The creation of tremendously engaging platform services that collectively concentrate power amongst the largest firms in the sector and limit competition over the consumer internet;

2.  Uninhibited collection of personal information that allows them to create behavior profiles on individual users without affording them control or access over their data; and

3.  The creation of highly sophisticated but opaque predictive algorithms that curate

Both Qu and Ghosh, respectively former Google and Facebook employees, termed such algorithms as potentially dangerous. Ghosh added that it is this precise business model that has generated negative externalities including the disinformation problem and the spread of hate speech, and that a triumvirate of corporate and regulatory policies could be considered to effectively respond to overextended companies that implicate the public's interest: consumer privacy, competition policy, and algorithmic transparency.

*Congressional Hearings Are Underutilized*

Apart from its legislative function, Congress holds an exploratory and investigative power through Congressional hearings. Congressional hearings played a crucial role in understanding and investigating both AT&T's corporate structure, as well as the cable industry in the 1990s. In both instances, Congress brought more information and expertise to the conversation, including insights from a broad spectrum of potential competitors, innovators, academics, and the public interest community. In describing the process leading up to the AT&T case settlement, Gene Kimmelman, former Chief Counsel for the U.S. Department of Justice's Antitrust Division, recalled that, "In 1981, the House Telecommunications subcommittee held 11 hearings in 6 months to put together a report." This report then served as the basis for both Senate and House bills.

However, Congressional hearings are being used less and less to inform the policy making process. There has been a notable decline in the number of hearings Congress holds. In the 1970s, Congress held roughly 6,000 hearings per year. By 1994, Congress held just over 4,000 hearings. Today, Congress holds just over 2,000 hearings annually.[2] In recent years, there has also been a marked shift in the way in which Congress utilizes the hearings they do hold. According to a 2015 study examining 40 years of committee hearings, sessions used to be used to solicit input from experts and explore potential policy solutions. The study found that today, however, hearings are more frequently used as a public communication tool to spotlight issues in a manner that is consistent with members' partisan leanings.[3] Not only are there substantially fewer hearings where Congress can leverage their exploratory and investigative power, but today's hearings are less frequently featuring substantive discussions to inform policy.

Among the event participants, there was widespread appetite to reverse this trend. Granular hearings, clearly tied back to the problem's definition and organized thematically, could increase policymaker awareness, hold companies accountable to the public interest, and better inform the American people. The importance of diverse perspectives in this process cannot be overstated. As Hong Qu, Program Director for Technology Shorenstein Center, noted, "In order to accomplish norms toward the public good, it needs to be a multi stakeholder process." A series of hearings would provide ample opportunity to allow consumers, workers, and industry representatives to voice their positions. In particular, when inviting companies, Congressional members should avoid only inviting C-level executives. The engineers and business managers, those who manage the company's day-to-day operations, will be particularly insightful in providing more technical and granular information on department-level business incentives, predictive models, and algorithms.

Throughout the event, the panelists and participants raised a variety of potential hearings topics, including but not limited to: an examination of big tech's data collection; how to define privacy; agency enforcement; algorithmic transparency and the impact on credit scores, housing, banking, employment, education, and the judicial system; the impact of foreign cyber regulatory regimes; data portability and social media; the impact of big tech on childhood development; and the risks of a decimated local news ecosystem.

## Today's Tech Debates Are Still "Pre-Partisan"

The issues of the Information Age—such as protecting consumer privacy, preventing disinformation campaigns, and non-competitive, overly concentrated markets—affect the constituents of each and every Congressional member. The nascent nature of today's debates over Big Tech and related policy issues presents a rare opportunity for healthy and honest partisan debate in service to the consent of the governed. From the Trump Administration's creation of an FTC competition task force to Senator Elizabeth Warren's "Breaking Up Big Tech" proposal, there is already interest to address these issues from both sides of the aisle.

The leadership for big tech policy solutions must reflect this reality through bipartisan engagement and a united front. As Toni Bush explained, "The important feature of the Cable Act of 1992 was that it was a bipartisan effort. In fact, it was the only successful veto override in the Bush administration." Likewise, the divestiture of AT&T began under Republican President Gerald Ford, continued under Democratic President Jimmy Carter, and came to a resolution under Republican President Ronald Reagan.

## Continuing the Conversation

The Belfer and Shorenstein Center's "Big Tech and Democracy" workshop fostered a space for congressional staffers to express their most-pressing concerns, inquiries and insights regarding tech policy issues. It added depth to the ongoing discussion of how to bring both policymakers and technical experts to the same table, undertake problem identification, and build a unified bipartisan front. The Belfer and Shorenstein Centers will continue to carry this momentum by providing additional resources to support congressional policy solutions. While an examination of past case studies built a foundation for discussion and policy frameworks, policymakers will need to consider a menu of technical, market-based, social, and regulatory solutions to adapt these historical observations into a blueprint for addressing today's tech marketplace.

### Endnotes

1. Venkat Alturi, Miklos Dietz, and Nicolaus Henke, "Competing in a world of sectors without borders," McKinsey Quarterly, July 2017. https://www.mckinsey.com/business-functions/mckinsey-analytics/our-insights/competing-in-a-world-of-sectors-without-borders#.

2. Pacrell Jr., Bill. "Why is Congress so dumb?" The Washington Post, January 11, 2019. https://www.washingtonpost.com/news/posteverything/wp/2019/01/11/feature/why-is-congress-so-dumb/?utm_term=.14d197b06a26.

3. Jonathan Lewallen et. al. "Congressional dysfunction: An information processing perspective," Regulation and Governance, May 8, 2015. https://onlinelibrary.wiley.com/doi/abs/10.1111/rego.12090.

# The Control of Big Tech on Democracy Must Be Stopped

*Sally Lee*

*Sally Lee is the editor in chief at* Columbia Magazine.

Columbia Law School professor Tim Wu, the expert who coined the term "net neutrality," calls for the breakup of big tech, big pharma, and big banks, and explains the consequences of excessive corporate power.

**Your latest book, The Curse of Bigness: Antitrust in the New Gilded Age, got a ton of press because it criticized big tech and called for the breakup of Facebook. Can you outline your argument?**

The premise of the book is that the US has become reluctant to enforce antitrust laws to their fullest extent and that, after forty years of allowing the unrestricted growth of certain industries, we are facing the consequences of excessive corporate power. As for Facebook, many of its acquisitions were, I suggest, in violation of the law. It bought its most dangerous main competitors, Instagram and WhatsApp, and should be dissolved.

**Were you surprised by the reaction to the book?**

Yes. I wouldn't say that the word "antitrust," at least in this century, is one that usually makes people's hearts beat with excitement. But then again, trusts and antitrust were once central to American politics. There were entire political parties organized around antitrust. The notion that power should be limited so that no person or institution can enjoy unaccountable influence is at the very root of our democracy.

Adapted from the article "How Big Tech is Crippling Democracy," by Sally Lee, first published in *Columbia Magazine*, Spring 2019. Reproduced with permission of *Columbia Magazine*. Copyright 2019 by Columbia University Trustees.

## Can you give us a brief history of trusts?

In the late nineteenth century there was a movement to reorganize the US economy into trusts, or monopolies. Proponents of trusts believed the economy should be centralized, free from government interference, and run by "great men," like J. P. Morgan and John D. Rockefeller. But the rising power of trusts, and the income inequalities they created, caused some concern, which led to the passage of the first antitrust law, the Sherman Act of 1890. That law was broad and wasn't really enforced, so I would say the true trustbusting tradition starts in 1901 with Theodore Roosevelt. He became president after the assassination of William McKinley, and he abruptly took the country in a very different economic direction. Within a year of his assuming the presidency, he filed suit against J. P. Morgan to prevent a merger that would have created a single western railroad. Roosevelt wanted to demonstrate the power of the federal government over a corporation and prove that the people were in charge. The case was close but, in the end, he won 5–4 in the Supreme Court and profoundly changed the course of American history.

Roosevelt then went after John D. Rockefeller and broke up the monopoly of the Standard Oil Company. In many ways, he was like the sheriff riding into town to protect the little guy. Since then we've had other people take up the antitrust mantle, including Taft—Roosevelt's successor—and Assistant Attorney General Thurman Arnold, who was an aggressive trustbuster at the height of the Great Depression. Most recently we had Joel Klein '67CC, '10HON, who was the lead prosecutor in the antitrust case against Microsoft in the 1990s. But it's been twenty years since there's been a case of real consequence. It's a powerful tool of American policy that we've lost.

## Many think of antitrust laws as a way to protect consumers. You consider them essential to a functioning democracy.

Absolutely. One of the goals of my book is to restore political and social understanding of the intent of the antitrust laws and to reinforce the idea that extreme corporate concentration is not only a threat to the economy but to the founding ideas of the American republic. One of the heroes of this book is Supreme Court justice Louis Brandeis, who, as a lawyer in the 1890s, saw the evils of monopolies and railed against the effect of what he called "excessive bigness" on small-business owners. He had a distinct vision for the economy, one rooted in his belief that America is the land of opportunity for the little guy, a place where everyone gets a fair shake. He saw the fight against the trust movement as a battle for the country's democratic soul.

Brandeis prompts us to think about what kind of country we want to live in and what kind of environment we want our government to provide for its citizens. I think those questions are more relevant than ever. Today we have massive income inequality, with the top 1 percent earning 23.8 percent of the national income and controlling 38.6 percent of the national wealth. I don't think it's the only contributor, but it stands to reason that industry concentration, with its greater shareholder returns and higher pay for executives, only widens the income gap. The workers' lack of bargaining power in these industries is another issue. Many people face the reality of being poorer than their parents. They're angry because they feel left behind. There's a general consensus that the extremist politics of our time, in the United States and around the globe, is tied to this sense of economic discontent.

### And there's historical precedent for your concerns about extremism.

There is. I think the history of the 1930s and the example of Italy, Germany, and Japan should not be forgotten. Economic dissatisfaction creates dangerous opportunities for political extremism. In the face of financial crisis, Germany turned to the Nazi Party, and German monopolists and industrialists played an important role in consolidating the power of Adolf Hitler and his hold over the German state.

**So should we consider ourselves warned?**

I hesitate before comparing President Trump to the dictators of the thirties, but there's no question that we are in a similar time. Trump rode a wave of economic dissatisfaction and anti-corporate populism to the presidency. He promised to make the country great again, to fight enemies foreign and domestic. In power he has shown a different stripe. He's erratic, random, and personal, which doesn't make him the greatest candidate to be a trustbuster.

**In your book you say Facebook has managed to string together sixty-seven unchallenged acquisitions, Amazon ninety-one, and Google 214 (a few of which had conditions). Why do these companies get a pass when it comes to buyouts?**

I think we are just coming to the end of a period in which many felt tech could do no wrong. Tech companies' business models did look different from those of, say, the cement industry, and so there was a feeling that they should be exempt from the normal rules. This rosy view of the industry, along with a fear that government interference in new technologies might kill the golden goose, motivated about ten years of softer treatment of tech both in the United States and in Europe.

**Are other industries enjoying this laissez-faire economic climate in a way that concerns you?**

Yes, absolutely. Tech has the highest visibility, but there are many industries that are far worse in my view. I can list four or five that have managed to consolidate in a way that I consider against the spirit of the antitrust laws. We have the US airline industry, where four companies control about 85 percent of traffic, leading to smaller seats, crowded planes, excessive fees, consumer abuse, you name it. We have the pharmaceutical industry, with its price-gouging practices. We have the global fertilizer and chemical industry, which has been allowed to merge down to just a few actors, and we have cable and telecom, where sixty-eight million Americans face a broadband monopolist. So many sectors have benefited.

**Let's focus on broadband. The FCC repealed net-neutrality rules in 2018. Maybe you could remind us what's at stake.**

Net neutrality stands for the proposition that the broadband networks, arguably today's most important infrastructure, should be subject to basic rules ensuring fair competition. Without net neutrality, carriers like Comcast and Verizon could restrict content and possibly block, speed up, or slow down traffic to impede competitors and to increase profits through paid prioritization. I'm sort of astonished that the FCC has eviscerated even those basic rules. This is one of the ways the Trump administration has been so disappointing.

**Recently Bayer, a huge European company, acquired Monsanto, a huge US company. How do antitrust laws work in a global economy?**

I think this is one of the most pressing challenges for the law over the next decade. Right now, the laws are not global: they're national or, in the case of Europe, regional. I don't see an easy answer. I think we have to figure something out or risk antitrust becoming a race to the bottom. There's no doubt that this is the fight of our times.

**Senator John Sherman, the author of the Sherman Antitrust Act of 1890, said, "The law of selfishness, uncontrolled by competition, compels [the trust] to disregard the interest of the consumer." Must big business, by its nature, be bad?**

Well, it's designed to put its own interests over human interests, to grow like a cancer, and to never die. I once heard someone say that if a corporation were a person, it would be a sociopath. Which brings us to the real question: who is this country for? For humans or these artificial entities?

**And sometimes antitrust action is good for business, yes?**

The old has to make way for the new. The breakup of the Bell System monopoly in the 1980s might have created chaos in the short term, but it did kickstart innovation. Without it we might not have gotten modems and home computing and the Internet revolution. And government scrutiny of IBM in the 1970s helped accelerate the personal-computing industry and the birth of independent software. I'd also say that Microsoft is a much more humanistic company than it once was, because it was policed by the government in the 1990s and went through a process of maturation. That's another benefit of antitrust actions: they play an important role in reasserting that people matter and people are in charge.

**You're a former adviser to the FTC, you were on President Obama's National Economic Council, and you ran for lieutenant governor of New York in 2014. Do you have another political run in your future?**

Let me think how to answer that. (Laughs.) I have no immediate plans to run for any office, but I do think that this is a time when academics should be engaged in the public discourse. It's also an important time for those in the academy, particularly in law and economics, to carefully examine our own work over the last forty years and ask whether we have made some serious mistakes. The academy plays a significant role in influencing elite opinion, and it can have a profound effect on the public good.

# Another Tech Is Possible

*Wolmet Barendregt, Christoph Becker, EunJeong Cheon, Andrew Clement, Pedro Reynolds-Cuéllar, Douglas Schuler, and Lucy Suchman*

*Wolmet Barendregt is with the Eindhoven University of Technology. Christoph Becker is affiliated with the University of Toronto. EunJeong Cheon is affiliated with Aalborg University. Andrew Clement is with the University of Toronto. Pedro Reynolds-Cuéllar is a PhD student at MIT Media Lab. Douglas Schuler is affiliated with Evergreen State College. Lucy Suchman is with Lancaster University.*

[…]

The origin myth of Big Tech is familiar to most of us: Risk-seeking genius entrepreneurs start from nothing and pursue a novel idea, from creation through commercialization and production to scale. According to the logic of this myth, the venture capitalists who, against all odds, followed their groundbreaking vision should reap the rewards: they created the value that fuels the revenue. But, as we explain below, very little of this familiar narrative is true. Its endless retelling only detracts from our ability to see both the challenges and opportunities that new communication technologies present.

First, the Big Tech "visionaries" invariably started with technologies based on research at institutions that rely on significant public funding. The venture capitalists did not take most of the risk, nor did the technologists create the basis for the market valuation of their developments on their own. Instead, as economist Mariana Mazzucato (2013) and others have shown, far from getting out of the way of private innovation the State paves the way. It is the State, not private capital, that funds the long-term, high-risk research and development (R&D) that underpins Big

Tech. Contrary to the reigning mythology, the State has not only generated the conditions that make Silicon Valley possible, it has also financed the R&D and in many cases supported its products up to the point of commercialization. Virtually every major technology that enables contemporary digital infrastructures, from the Internet itself to the now iconic smartphone, was created by nationally funded R&D long before the technology came to market.

Second, despite its pivotal role the State has been systematically deprived of the rewards generated from its own innovation investments. Decades of lobbying for deregulation have allowed companies like Apple to avoid "paying back" a share of their profits to the same State that funded much of their success. The Big Five exploit their clout to avoid paying billions of dollars in taxes, as well as fines when found guilty of offenses. In the end, the State is left with a tail of complex issues to deal with.

Finally, Big Tech companies are so highly profitable because they generate economic value at enormous scale. But who creates much of that value? Users. Facebook and Google sell user profiles, composed of content that was created by their users—not the company. What has value in a user profile is not the data structure, but the record of choices that users make and the content that they create. These choices, and the attention required to produce and consume them, become valuable assets for the platforms to sell to advertisers. Everything else facilitates that value's extraction and monetization. In the case of Facebook, the company has secured a monopoly on the monetization of the value created by its users and prevents that from being shared more freely. Platforms such as Twitter and Instagram similarly rely entirely on their users to create the value that makes other users engage. All of these digital spaces are permeated by ceaseless advertisement. The labor of users in creating the value of these platforms can easily be counted in the engagement metrics that companies compile. To further complicate matters, the infrastructures that enable a significant proportion of the value of Big Tech's key services rest on the shoulders of an extractive, underpaid, wide network of invisible labor, which has created a significant proportion of the value at the core of several of Big Tech's key services. A parallel situation plays out in the gig economy, in which workers are beholden to platform companies for uncertain, insecure, and temporary employment. This pipeline of labor is deeply problematic: its globally—and vastly unequally—distributed nature, across what Virginia Eubanks calls "low-rights environments," creates the conditions for a vulnerable workforce with virtually no legal frameworks for advocacy or protection. On top of that, this already troubling system is not exempt from the racial and colonial shadows of the past. From the racialization of women of color within the production pipeline of early electronics, to the ethnic stereotyping of South Indian workers as fit for technology-related work, the foundations of value creation of Big Tech, and Silicon Valley more widely, inherit the legacies of racial capitalism.

So, what is the problem with all of this? At first sight, the rapid growth of Big Tech indicates that these technologies are meeting some societal needs. In just a few decades, Big Tech has become part of the daily life of billions around the globe. Yet the social costs of this approach to digital infrastructure and services are far less visible. Driven by a handful of individuals and shareholder imperatives, the Big Five are de facto monopolists, integrated both vertically and horizontally, positioning themselves as unavoidable gatekeepers in their respective areas of specialization. This market dominance has brought on multiple anti-trust investigations, by the US Congress, the Attorneys General of 50 US states and territories, and the EU.

But the greatest threats that Big Tech wealth poses are to democracy. Similar to earlier historical periods when high concentrations of wealth threatened democratic practices, Big Tech companies use their economic power across a wide spectrum of political arenas. They are among the most active lobbyists in the communications and electronics sector, pushing the passage of laws in their favor or resisting those that aren't. Brazenly pressing governments for their private gain over public interests, they are often powerful enough to get away with it. In areas where regulation is weak or non-existent, they charge ahead with a "catch me if you can" approach. Given the relative novelty of their technological foundations and associated business models, key aspects of Big Tech operations are often arguably at the margins of or even outside conventional legal jurisdictions and regulatory regimes. Foremost within the tech industry, the Big Five typically claim that any constraint on their actions would 'stifle innovation,' threatening vague but ominous societal costs. They conveniently ignore the possibility that their innovations may be harmful and too often are.

As many have pointed out, the fine-grained capture, analysis and exploitation of personal information to influence behavior on a population-wide scale in the pursuit of private commercial interests constitutes a dangerous form of what scholar Shoshana Zuboff (2018) refers to as "surveillance capitalism." Monetizing the personal information and attention of their users has proven to be so lucrative for advertising-reliant tech companies that they have gone beyond developing features that provide value for users and have systematically designed their services to be "addictive." Employing techniques from behavioral psychology that operate subconsciously, these companies "hook" people into acting in ways that serve their commercial advantage. This can have deleterious effects for the individuals concerned, eroding their agency and autonomy. Most notably, these practices have contributed to people being subjected to political manipulation.

In addition to the familiar ways in which large corporations have long sought to influence political processes, Big Tech's novel business models, which rely to varying degrees on exploiting the personal information and communications of their users, introduce new openings for the disruption of conventional governance. The most prominent example is the controversy over the damaging role that social media plays in elections, witnessed recently with the storming of the United States Capitol. Facebook is currently the biggest public villain, tarred with the Cambridge Analytica scandal and for enabling hateful speech and inflammatory (mis) information to circulate widely and rapidly on its networks, especially during contentious elections.

To compound the problems of mass surveillance, rather than reining in Big Tech's bulk collection and exploitation of personal information, governments have sought to take advantage of their massive data stores and big-data analytic capabilities for State security intelligence purposes, foreign and domestic. As Edward Snowden has revealed, the US National Security Agency (NSA) has taken the lead in this regard. Its PRISM surveillance program, in which at least four of the Big Five companies formally participated, was reportedly "the number one source of raw intelligence used for NSA analytic reports."

One disturbing result of Big Tech's infrastructures becoming an arm of the state is the use of pervasive surveillance to exacerbate the long-term mass incarceration crisis in the United States. Facial recognition, predictive policing and risk profiling algorithms, among other carceral technologies, serve as mechanisms that reproduce a long history of racial policing and discrimination both in the United States and abroad. These technologies are leveraged as weapons "used by law enforcement to identify, profile, and enact violence against categories of people" (Hamid, 2020). These techniques are further fine-tuned and normalized through unwitting participation of the public via consumer products, such as biometric identification on smartphones.

There are further, less direct but no less potent ways that Big Tech enterprises play an outsized role in governance. As forceful promoters of technological solutionism, prioritizing technological answers to a broad range of social, economic, political and environmental questions facing contemporary society, they marginalize less intensively technological but possibly more appropriate responses. Even where digital technologies can play an appropriate role, Big Tech overly constrains the viable options. For example, instead of treating personal information captured during on-line interactions exclusively as a proprietary corporate asset to be monetized in various ways, with appropriate consideration of subject rights, that information could be viewed as a collective or common asset, to be managed through data trusts or cooperatives for public benefit.

Big Tech companies that rely on advertising erode democratic governance as well in their undermining of an indispensable feature of democratic deliberation, independent professional journalism. As Google and Facebook capture a large and growing proportion of advertising revenues, they deprive conventional news media of the income that supports their reporting and they typically refuse to underwrite the cost of producing the news content that attracts people to their platforms. Moreover they allow users to post excerpts of news on their platforms without properly compensating publishers. As a result, publishers' find themselves drawn into an advertising business model that has serious consequences for independent journalism, and in which the news media that have safeguarded democracy for centuries are starving.

In sum, Big Tech has shown that digital technologies can offer significant social value, but in a remarkably short period of time the industry has also developed practices that now threaten the capabilities of democratic governance. This brings us to our call for defunding, to ensure that digital technology serves the public interest.

## Defunding Big Tech

In the spirit of the anti-racist defund campaign, we propose to extend the project of resource redistribution to the domain of public infrastructures, and more specifically to the processes through which vital information and communication technologies are developed. In keeping with Ron Deibert's (2020) and Cory Doctorow's (2020) recent calls to restrain the forces of surveillance capitalism, we focus first on curtailing the power of Big Tech, while recovering resources currently contributing to its hold on our information and communications infrastructure (defund), which can then be redirected to community-oriented services (refund).

These changes will require initiatives on the part of multiple actors, starting with Big Tech itself.

## Big Tech (and other tech businesses)

The major tech companies need to take seriously the legitimate concerns about their excessive power and harmful impacts increasingly being voiced by actors across the social, political and economic spectrum. In particular, Big Tech companies need to:

- Pay their fair share of taxes. Lost revenues through tax avoidance by Silicon Valley's largest companies (Facebook, Apple, Amazon, Netflix, Google and Microsoft) exceed $100bn globally over the past ten years.
- Stop secretive lobbying and other behind-the-scenes efforts to prevent regulation. While some degree of lobbying is legitimate, it must be conducted in full public view.
- Provide public transparency regarding privacy policy, surveillance practices, data trafficking, political campaigning on social media, and environmental impacts (energy consumption and sources).
- Offer API (Application Programming Interface) access to core functions compliant with open standards to enable interoperability with alternate service providers.
- Support the right to repair. If we cannot sustain the functioning of our devices, we cannot ensure they are used to the full.

History has proven that Big Tech will not take these measures simply on their own initiative. Collective action on the part of civil society and government will be required to exert the pressure and regulatory force that can reshape Big Tech priorities and modes of operation.

## Governments and Policymakers

Government has the primary responsibility to promote the public interest, as well as being the only institution with enough legitimacy, authority and resources to hold Big Tech to account, especially to the degree that it works in concert with civil society. Elected public bodies must act decisively and collaboratively across jurisdictions to regulate Big Tech, require those corporations to pay fair taxes, and through their procurement and contracting powers foster a tech sector that sustainably meets people's information and communication needs. In particular, governments and policymakers need to:

- Revive antitrust laws to break up monopolies and uncouple anti-competitive mergers, to enable more competitive markets and rein in excessive political influence.
- Designate large tech platforms as "Platform Utilities," prohibiting Big Tech from owning and monetizing both the platform and its users.
- Require platform interoperability, including to facilitate "identity portability" to enable alternative business models, including non-profit ones, to emerge without holding users captive.
- Extend producer responsibility to mitigate environmental harms and to support repair versus planned obsolescence.
- Establish and enforce a reasonable tax regime based on out-sized corporate profits or financial transactions or both, as well as other approaches that refund community.
- Roll back mass state surveillance, particularly where it depends on secret and unaccountable government access to personal data held by platform providers.
- Establish strong international privacy and other digital rights regimes, robust enough to effectively protect individuals as well as to help abolish the surveillance capitalism business model.
- Reduce dependence of public institutions on Big Tech. Across several sectors, notably defense, government services and education, governments have come to rely heavily on Big Tech services, making it harder to rein in their excesses. Instead, public institutions could leverage their collective power in order to develop their own services, or support the

development of alternative community-governed services that are not controlled by Big Tech.

- Consult and collaborate with professional organizations, like the Association for Computing Machinery (ACM), workers and organized labor, advocacy and human rights groups, environmental groups and others to ensure that all voices are heard and that important local knowledge is considered when developing tech policy.
- Consult and collaborate with other governmental bodies, including towns, cities, and regional as well as national, international, and supranational bodies to help ensure that fair, prudent, and non oppressive digital policies are not just enjoyed by a privileged few.

## Tech Professionals/Workers, Researchers and Their Organizations

As the people most knowledgeable about Big Tech operations, as well as those workers whose labors are essential for Big Tech's ongoing viability, tech workers have an especially important, transformative role to play. Many entered the industry with high expectations about the contributions they could make to social betterment, but have since become disillusioned. While tech researchers are more removed from operations, they too can offer well-informed insights. Working together, these groups need to:

- Organize to oppose egregious Big Tech behaviour, drawing on already successful efforts.
- Refuse sponsorships from companies violating criteria for good business practices.
- Work within professional organizations to ensure that these issues get the attention they deserve.
- Educate technology students about the dangers of Big Tech and how to take responsibility for the systems that they develop.
- Support professionals worldwide who bring tech abuses to light and encourage community tech.

- Use their technological expertise and social imagination to work with people in the community as well as with government officials and civil society organizations, to envision, design, build, and manage alternatives to Big Tech and other mainstream corporate approaches.

## *Civil Society Organizations and Social Movements*

It is often civil society organizations (CSOs) and social movements that lead governments to act in the interests of the people they are supposed to serve, and then keep pushing to ensure that they do the right thing. They act as expert watchdogs, policy entrepreneurs and a primary vehicle for effective mobilizing, pressuring corporations and governments into action. While there are many CSOs active in the tech/digital rights field, so far there is not the same degree of social movement mobilization that other areas, such as racial justice and environmental sustainability, have attained. Here are some actions that could be taken:

- Closely monitor Big Tech and hold it to account in such areas as market competition, civil liberties, accessibility, labor and environmental sustainability.
- Consider alternatives to Big Tech platforms for communicating with supporters, organizing events, and publicizing issues.
- Cooperate with community members, tech workers, and others in developing and implementing approaches that improve the effectiveness of their efforts without sacrificing their ideals.
- Work with other organizations and networks around the world to ensure that tech companies and governments are using tech responsibly.

## *We As Individuals (Consumers, Business, Investors)*

If we want to abolish the conditions that lead to Big Tech harms while redirecting technology development towards a more just and sustainable future, individual actions, however small, that are commensurate with our skills, means and fields of expertise can cumulatively contribute to significant changes. Many of us are in a position to withhold both the personal information and money that Big Tech relies on, and to re-direct them more positively. Here are some steps to take, which are more effective when made in concert and collectively:

- Insist that governments serve their role as defenders of human rights and advocates for the public interest in pursuing the actions identified above, as without this pressure they will likely fail to do so.
- Recognize that no computing comes without cost, even when offered "for free." We pay collectively for advertising supported services through higher consumer prices. As noted above, we need to consider a host of other hidden costs as well, in terms of democracy, privacy and other civil liberties, and environmental sustainability.
- Resist Big Tech surveillance practices, by using alternative, preferably open source services for search, browsing, emailing, messaging, video conferencing, ad blocking, and web tracker blocking, and mapping.
- Boycott advertising on Facebook and other platforms that harm democracy and otherwise act egregiously against the public interest.
- Subscribe to, and when feasible pay for, high quality journalism and other informational resources, rather than simply accessing them through platforms that redistribute content for free without fairly compensating the source.
- Support and work with civil society organizations in their anti-surveillance efforts and other efforts to shape democratic technology.
- Exercise our democratic rights and responsibilities, e.g. freedoms of expression, communication, privacy, and assembly.

There is growing public support for reining in the power of Big Tech. Anti-trust initiatives are leading the way, with the goal of breaking up the giants and better regulating the industry. However, while these are urgent, vital measures, we need to look well beyond simply allowing the Big Five's smaller competitors to participate in digital markets that remain driven by conventional business models. There is currently a rare window of opportunity to consider how these enormous revenue flows can be put to re-orienting technology development to better serve much wider societal aims.

## Refunding Community

The principal purpose of defunding Big Tech is to reduce its out-sized power and redirect its excessive revenue flows toward better serving human needs. There are many entangled areas of societal crisis that call for priority treatment, including the climate emergency and environmental protection, democratic reform, social in/equality (e.g. resolving economic, class, racial, gender disparities), and criminal justice reform, to name the most prominent. Without challenging these vital claims for resources, we focus here on technology developments aimed at meeting people's diverse information and communication needs while remaining under community control. We refer to this broadly as community tech.

[…]

Refunding community implies assuming greater shared responsibility for all aspects of the technology life-cycle, from concept and design to deployment, redesign, repair and retirement. All refunding community work should consider education as part of its mission, including how technology works and how to work with it, but also critical thinking with respect to its social implications. This includes identifying and communicating the real costs of tech and potential future harms, and sponsoring conversations around tech workers and working conditions.

There are now thousands of new projects that support various aspects of democratic decision-making including discussion, deliberation, service design, information sharing, local news aggregation, DIY media, decision-making, environmental monitoring, government transparency, and participatory budgeting. One of the challenges is providing the resources and the institutional infrastructure to keep these projects thriving. The City of Seattle, for example, established a Citizens Advisory Board on Technology (CTAB) that, among other duties, makes small grants to neighborhood tech projects. At a larger scale a Corporation for Public Software entity has recently been proposed that would help ensure that public software, especially deliberative systems, would find a secure place in the public sphere. Civic hacking events develop public data and digital applications for civic uses. The Ideas for Change consultancy has developed large EU projects that use participatory design and digital technology such as sensing technology to help people take an active role in improving their city. Barcelona, Spain, is home to a wide variety of innovative community and civic tech projects including Barcelona Ciutat Refugi (Barcelona Refugee City) to help address the humanitarian crisis of millions of displaced people.

At the same time, grand initiatives by Big Tech players to make cities or regions 'smart' deserve critical scrutiny, especially proposals that sideline residents. Some of these efforts attempt to shift important public responsibilities into private hands. Many make impossibly confident claims, provide minimal transparency, and hoard public data for their private gain. Local resident organizing has in some cases been effective in halting such projects and opening up possibilities for more genuinely participatory urban planning that takes advantage of digital technologies in ways that reflect local resident needs and aspirations.

One notable effort offering freedom from Big Tech domination is DECIDIM, a free and open source system for a variety of participatory governance approaches, which is now being used or tested in cities around the world including Barcelona, Milan, Helsinki, and Mexico City. Moreover, groups and governments around the world such as the International Federation of Red Cross and Red Crescent Societies are working to share data to help implement smart systems for the common good. Recent proposals on the development of data cooperatives, trusts and stewardship models are paving the way to community-first data paradigms. Some have recently developed technology in ways that benefit communities, such as Sentilo and DECODE in Barcelona, which focus on urban sensors and making data generated available for public benefit, or Telecomunicaciones Indigenas Comunitarias focused on public communications infrastructure in México. Others such as Free Geek and Reboot Canada focus on recycling hardware to help provide affordable computing in communities promoting a range of social equity goals. We Don't Have Time is a movement and a tech startup that leverages the power of social media to hold leaders and companies accountable for climate change. Many other community tech initiatives worthy of support could be mentioned.

Where conventional forms of democratic decision-making are found inadequate for tackling thorny policy challenges, such as the climate crisis and electoral reform, people have turned to citizens' assemblies as a more popular form of collective deliberation around controversial issues. Citizens' assemblies may also be suitable for proposing, assessing and recommending strategies for technology development that can be relatively free of the Influence of Big Tech interests and technological solutionism more generally. Even more modest public forums, such as debates between contending advocates and questioning of experts, can help people to understand the technological options and limitations of technological solutions for issues of concern, otherwise obscured by Big Tech promotions.

[...]

# Research Shows That Regulation by Big Tech Can Be Effective

*Anjana Susarla*

*Anjana Susarla is a professor of responsible AI at Michigan State University.*

Governments and observers across the world have repeatedly raised concerns about the monopoly power of Big Tech companies and the role the companies play in disseminating misinformation. In response, Big Tech companies have tried to preempt regulations by regulating themselves.

With Facebook's announcement that its Oversight Board will make a decision about whether former President Donald Trump can regain access to his account after the company suspended it, this and other high-profile moves by technology companies to address misinformation have reignited the debate about what responsible self-regulation by technology companies should look like.

Research shows three key ways social media self-regulation can work: deprioritize engagement, label misinformation and crowdsource accuracy verification.

## Deprioritize Engagement

Social media platforms are built for constant interaction, and the companies design the algorithms that choose which posts people see to keep their users engaged. Studies show falsehoods spread faster than truth on social media, often because people find news that triggers emotions to be more engaging, which makes it more likely they will read, react to and share such news. This effect gets amplified through algorithmic recommendations.

My own work shows that people engage with YouTube videos about diabetes more often when the videos are less informative.

Most Big Tech platforms also operate without the gatekeepers or filters that govern traditional sources of news and information. Their vast troves of fine-grained and detailed demographic data give them the ability to "microtarget" small numbers of users. This, combined with algorithmic amplification of content designed to boost engagement, can have a host of negative consequences for society, including digital voter suppression, the targeting of minorities for disinformation and discriminatory ad targeting.

Deprioritizing engagement in content recommendations should lessen the "rabbit hole" effect of social media, where people look at post after post, video after video. The algorithmic design of Big Tech platforms prioritizes new and microtargeted content, which fosters an almost unchecked proliferation of misinformation. Apple CEO Tim Cook recently summed up the problem: "At a moment of rampant disinformation and conspiracy theories juiced by algorithms, we can no longer turn a blind eye to a theory of technology that says all engagement is good engagement—the longer the better—and all with the goal of collecting as much data as possible."

## Label Misinformation

The technology companies could adopt a content-labeling system to identify whether a news item is verified or not. During the election, Twitter announced a civic integrity policy under which tweets labeled as disputed or misleading would not be recommended by their algorithms. Research shows that labeling works. Studies suggest that applying labels to posts from state-controlled media outlets, such as from the Russian media channel RT, could mitigate the effects of misinformation.

In an experiment, researchers hired anonymous temporary workers to label trustworthy posts. The posts were subsequently displayed on Facebook with labels annotated by the crowdsource workers. In that experiment, crowd workers from across the political spectrum were able to distinguish between mainstream sources and hyperpartisan or fake news sources, suggesting that crowds often do a good job of telling the difference between real and fake news.

Experiments also show that individuals with some exposure to news sources can generally distinguish between real and fake news. Other experiments found that providing a reminder about the accuracy of a post increased the likelihood that participants shared accurate posts more than inaccurate posts.

In my own work, I have studied how combinations of human annotators, or content moderators, and artificial intelligence algorithms—what is referred to as human-in-the-loop intelligence—can be used to classify health care-related videos on YouTube. While it is not feasible to have medical professionals watch every single YouTube video on diabetes, it is possible to have a human-in-the-loop method of classification. For example, my colleagues and I recruited subject-matter experts to give feedback to AI algorithms, which results in better assessments of the content of posts and videos.

Tech companies have already employed such approaches. Facebook uses a combination of fact-checkers and similarity-detection algorithms to screen COVID-19-related misinformation. The algorithms detect duplications and close copies of misleading posts.

## Community-Based Enforcement

Twitter recently announced that it is launching a community forum, Birdwatch, to combat misinformation. While Twitter hasn't provided details about how this will be implemented, a crowd-based verification mechanism adding up votes or down votes to trending posts and using newsfeed algorithms to down-rank content from untrustworthy sources could help reduce misinformation.

The basic idea is similar to Wikipedia's content contribution system, where volunteers classify whether trending posts are real or fake. The challenge is preventing people from up-voting interesting and compelling but unverified content, particularly when there are deliberate efforts to manipulate voting. People can game the systems through coordinated action, as in the recent GameStop stock-pumping episode.

Another problem is how to motivate people to voluntarily participate in a collaborative effort such as crowdsourced fake news detection. Such efforts, however, rely on volunteers annotating the accuracy of news articles, akin to Wikipedia, and also require the participation of third-party fact-checking organizations that can be used to detect if a piece of news is misleading.

However, a Wikipedia-style model needs robust mechanisms of community governance to ensure that individual volunteers follow consistent guidelines when they authenticate and fact-check posts. Wikipedia recently updated its community standards specifically to stem the spread of misinformation. Whether the big-tech companies will voluntarily allow their content moderation policies to be reviewed so transparently is another matter.

## Big Tech's Responsibilities

Ultimately, social media companies could use a combination of deprioritizing engagement, partnering with news organizations, and AI and crowdsourced misinformation detection. These approaches are unlikely to work in isolation and will need to be designed to work together.

Coordinated actions facilitated by social media can disrupt society, from financial markets to politics. The technology platforms play an extraordinarily large role in shaping public opinion, which means they bear a responsibility to the public to govern themselves effectively.

Calls for government regulation of Big Tech are growing all over the world, including in the U.S., where a recent Gallup poll showed worsening attitudes toward technology companies and greater support for governmental regulation. Germany's new laws on content moderation push greater responsibility on tech companies for the content shared on their platforms. A slew of regulations in Europe aimed at reducing the liability protections enjoyed by these platforms and proposed regulations in the U.S. aimed at restructuring internet laws will bring greater scrutiny to tech companies' content moderation policies.

Some form of government regulation is likely in the U.S. Big Tech still has an opportunity to engage in responsible self-regulation—before the companies are compelled to act by lawmakers.

# Big Tech Is Worth Fixing

*Shaoul Sussman*

*Shaoul Sussman is a legal fellow and researcher focusing on antitrust law and big tech. Sussman has published an academic paper and articles about the anticompetitive practices at Amazon.*

Apologists for Big Tech lost a crucial battle last week. They have failed to persuade a single member of the Congressional Antitrust Subcommittee that nothing was wrong with the tech goliaths and that legislative intervention was unnecessary.

This failure is all the more spectacular considering the scope of the lobbying endeavor; a long, expensive, and concentrated effort to sway elected representatives that included the emergency circulation of a talking points memo in a last-ditch effort to turn the tide.

It is important to recognize the monumental shift in the public debate surrounding Big Tech. The question presented to our elected officials is no longer whether tech giants are monopolies, or whether these monopolies are harmful, but rather what should Congress do about this significant and harmful market failure.

And although much-deserved attention was given to parsing out any incriminating statements made with respect to particular examples of self-preferencing, monopoly leveraging, and general anticompetitive conduct, the Congressional hearing has been extremely informative in another, less obvious respect: the answers that the four tech CEOs provided in response to the precise and piercing questions volleyed by the members of the subcommittee could now inform Congress in determining the correct course of remedial legislative action.

During his opening statement, Rep. Sensenbrenner (R-WI) remarked that "Being big is not inherently bad. Quite the opposite.

"Big Tech Is Officially Too Big to Manage," by Shaoul Sussman, Promarket, August 5, 2020. Reprinted by permission.

In America, you should be rewarded for success." But if anything, the hearing proved the opposite. It not only cemented the consensus on Capitol Hill that the four major tech platforms are harmful to free markets but also the realization that, due to their gargantuan size, these companies appear to be cobbled amalgamations of various lines of business that are too big to manage as one firm.

This point was demonstrated with resounding clarity when one particular answer was constantly and repeatedly dished out by all four CEOs: "I don't know about that…" or "Congresswoman, I don't know."

That particular phrase was utilized frequently by the grilled executives on multiple occasions. And when the questioning Congressmember insisted on an explanation or clarification for this lack of knowledge, the typical answer was "I wasn't very involved."

There is no question that at least some of these answers were motivated by a desire to avoid making incriminating statements, but it is also clear that in some cases the professed lack of knowledge was genuine and sincere.

For example, Rep. Kelly Armstong (R-ND) asked Amazon CEO Jeff Bezos a benign question: "My understanding is that Twitch, a video live streaming service that has nothing to do with Amazon's other lines of business of cloud computing or e-commerce, allows users to stream music, but does not license the music. Is that correct?" Bezos' answer was "I'm going to have to ask that I could get back to your office with an answer to that question. I don't know." It is doubtful that the CEO of a company that focused exclusively on video streaming would have not known the answer.

In other cases, this lack of knowledge, even if true, was extremely troubling.

For example, Rep. Hank Johnson (D-GA) asked Apple CEO Tim Cook whether some developers are favored over others in Apple's App Store. Cook first replied, "That is not correct." Johnson then moved on to provide an example: "Baidu has two App Store employees assigned to help it navigate the App Store bureaucracy. Is that true?" Cook's reply was "I don't know about that, sir."

Similarly, Rep. Mary Gay Scanlon (D-PA) mentioned reports that Amazon continued to ship Amazon-branded products during the pandemic despite the company's statement that it would only ship essential items, and asked Bezos if this was true. "I don't know the answer to that question," Bezos replied.

These examples explain a lot about the corporate culture at these colossal amalgamated firms. It appears that executives push middle management to achieve growth by all means necessary while putting in place policies that are supposed to protect against anticompetitive conduct or abuse but are, in reality, a dead letter frequently trampled on in pursuit of "growth" or "results."

The hearing exposed the harms that bigness and corporate concentration bring about. The question remains whether a legislative remedy would address this problem. That is, whether Congress will realize that the US is facing not just a" competition breakdown" but also markets plagued by monopolization and corporate concentration.

## Congress' Failure to Curb Western Union's Monopoly and Today's Big Tech

Congress has already failed to pass remedial legislation of a similar nature once before, assuming instead that corporate concentration in a broken market was inevitable and that a dominant company—in this case, Western Union—merely lacked competitors.

In his masterful historical monograph *Network Nation: Inventing American Telecommunications*, Columbia professor Richard R. John has carefully documented Congress' abortive attempts to fight Western Union's monopoly power. On two occasions, in 1866 and 1879 Congress passed legislation aimed at propping up rivals that would compete with Western Unions' dominance. But both attempts failed. In fact, as John demonstrates, they actually helped Robber Baron Jay Gould to take over the company in 1881. After the takeover, the frustration with Western Union on Capitol Hill was unanimous, and a bipartisan agreement emerged among members of Congress that they should, for the third time in 20 years, pass legislation to curtail Western Union's monopoly over the telegraph business.

This bipartisan agreement greatly resembles today's rare agreement between Republicans and Democrats that Congress should act to regulate Big Tech. Back then, however, Congress failed.

As John's work reveals, the prevailing notion among members of Congress throughout the period was that size mattered, and that breaking up the company would greatly harm the telegraph industry. (Although Western Union in the 1880s remained the loosely-structured horizontal combine and was referred to as a collectivity—that is, as "the Western Union," rather than simply as "Western Union.").

Since breaking up Western Union was off the table, two alternative proposals were floated on Capitol Hill. The first, a government buyout (which was advocated for since the late 1860s) that would nationalize the telegraph industry and transfer its management to a government-run corporation or the post office. The second: attempt to prop up—for the third time—a large private corporation that could rival Western Union's size and inject competition into the monopolized market.

These two competing solutions gave rise to competing political factions, each viewing the other's solution as inadequate and even disastrous. A government buyout angered the proponents of free-markets and private enterprise, while the propping up of private rivals raised real concerns of corruption and nepotism in light of Gould's past maneuverings. Congress ultimately arrived at a deadlock. It was determined to create competition but was hesitant to break up corporate concentration.

Congress' legislative stalemate regarding Western Union is even more remarkable given the pace and decisiveness with which State attorneys general moved to break up the monopolies of the time.

Frank William Taussig, a prominent Harvard economist who reflected on the events of that period thirty years later, argued that one of the biggest general fallacies adopted at the close of the century was that "Legislation cannot prevent monopoly, nor can it prevent its concomitant of ever-growing inequality."

It seems that then, as today, many Big Tech promoters and detractors presupposed that the size of these corporations is an essential feature in the deployment of the innovative technology services they provide. In light of presuppositions, some critics on the left today support the nationalization of Amazon or Facebook, while defenders of the tech platforms insist that even a slight disturbance of the status quo would be disastrous for the digital economy.

These voices are eerily reminiscent of positions held during the feverish efforts of the 1880s to nationalize Western Union. Today, as in the 1880s, the dogma underlying this view is that these firms employ cutting-edge technologies that can only be utilized effectively on a grand scale.

In his 1921 treatise The Financial Policy of Corporations, Arthur Stone Dewing, who was by no means a socialist or even a progressive, reflected that the public antimonopoly debate during the 1880s and 90s was plagued by the false belief that "bigger is better" and that all sectors of the economy are doomed to consolidate in a Darwinian process of brutal corporate natural selection.

Foremost in Dewing's analysis was the inherent diffusion of responsibility in giant corporations. As he bluntly put it: "There comes a point where the man in the twentieth story of an office building cannot make up, no matter how brilliant he may be, for the waste and shiftlessness of a variety of superintendents in many mills hundreds of miles away in all directions". Anecdotal evidence shows the same problem plaguing the giant tech corporations of today.

Dewing's observations can be easily applied to the performance of the Tech CEOs during last week's hearing. Even if Zuckerberg, Cook, Pichai, and Bezos are truly trying to manage their sprawling digital kingdoms as if they were a single firm, it's become abundantly clear that the enormous detail involved is too great a burden for a single mind. It was clear that important matters passed unnoticed, and that middle management, using Dewing's own words "degenerated into automatic parts of a machine, without initiative or power of assuming responsibility."

Dewing went on to conclude that hard evidence "tends to show that large-scale production is not of itself necessarily economical, and if large-scale production is not necessarily economical, to show that it is inevitable is difficult."

Dewing's conclusions, although made 100 years ago about events that took place 40 years before then, are supported by a recent report published by Institute of Local Self Reliance [the author is a Fellow at the ILSR] that found that between 2013 and 2019, the standard rate for storing inventory in Amazon's warehouses during off-peak months rose 67 percent. And that storage rates for standard-sized items (those under 20 pounds and within certain dimensions) are now 75 cents per cubic foot per month during the first part of the year and $2.40 during the peak season.

Most notably, Amazon's storage fees are much higher than those of its competitors, according to several sources. A 2019 survey of 600 warehouses across the US and Canada, for example, found an average rate of only 50 cents per cubic foot.

If we assume that Amazon does not charge monopoly rents for these services, which Amazon will argue it doesn't, the increase in fees must demonstrate that Amazon has become less efficient. That is, Amazon's growth rendered it less efficient in storing goods, and at this point the prices it charges the consumers of its storage services are much higher than the national average.

Last week, Congress made history when it uniformly took the stance that Big Tech is a threat to American democracy and free markets. But in order to achieve its goal of successfully curbing the monopoly power of the big tech platforms, Congress must first reject the presupposition that bigger is necessarily better and perceive that breakups, which reduce corporate concentration—as opposed to nationalization or the propping up of large competitors—would be the most expedient legislative solution.

# Organizations to Contact

*The editors have compiled the following list of organizations concerned with the issues debated in this book. The descriptions are derived from materials provided by the organizations. All have publications or information available for interested readers. This list was compiled on the date of publication of the present volume; the information provided here may change. Be aware that many organizations take several weeks or longer to respond to inquiries, so allow as much time as possible.*

### Brookings Institute
1775 Massachusetts Avenue NW, Washington, DC 20036
(207) 797-6000
email: use links on contact page
website: www.brookings.edu/

The Brookings Institute is a nonprofit public policy organization dedicated to finding solutions through research at the federal, state, and local level. Gain insight into big tech through articles, podcasts, blogs, and published materials.

### CATO Institute
1000 Massachusetts Avenue NW, Washington, DC 20001-5403
(202) 842-0200
email: use form on contact page
website: www.cato.org/

The Cato Institute is a public policy research organization dedicated to a free, open, and civil society. Read articles, follow their blog, sign up for a newsletter. Find lots of information and information on the issues surrounding big tech.

## Center For Cybersecurity (CCS)

370 Jay Street, 10<sup>th</sup> Floor
Brooklyn, NY 11201
(646) 997-3671
email: ccs@nyu.edu
website: cyber.nyu.edu

The Center For Cybersecurity is a research institute dedicated to training current and future cybersecurity professionals. Read about interesting research and press releases including information on the risks of apps on iPhones. Join their newsletter to stay up to date on current cybersecurity events.

## Electronic Frontier Foundation (EFF)

815 Eddy Street
San Francisco, CA 94109
(415) 436-9333
email: info@eff.org
website: www.eff.org

The Electronic Frontier Foundation is the leading nonprofit organization dedicated to fighting for digital liberty. They champion issues related to big tech—free speech online, illegal surveillance, advocacy for users, and support of freedom enhancing technologies. Stay current on technology by following their blog and sign up for their newsletter.

## Heritage Foundation

214 Massachusetts Avenue NE
Washington, DC 20002-4999
(800) 546-2843
email: info@heritage.org
website: www.heritage.org/

The Heritage Foundation has a mission to promote conservative policies and traditional American values. Find a wealth of information about big tech here. Read the news, link to featured videos, and listen to podcasts.

## London School of Economics (LSE)

Houghton Street
WC2A 2AE
London, UK
+44 (0)20 7405 7686
email: use links on contact page
website: www.lse.ac.uk/

Visit the London School of Economics site to uncover a wide range of information on important topics. Explore their vlogs, blogs, podcasts, and videos. Students from all over the world attain advanced degrees at this university.

## Organization for Economic Cooperation and Development (OECD)

1776 Eye Street NW, Suite 450
Washington, DC 20009
(202) 785-6323
email: washington.contact@oecd.org
website: www.oecd.org/washington/

The OECD is an international organization dedicated to building better lives for all citizens across the globe. This site has a variety of online tools to explore current issues including a data portal and an iLibrary.

## Warren

Warren Democrats, PO Box 171375
Boston, MA 02117
email: use links on contact page
website: www.2020.elizabethwarren.com/

Senator Elizabeth Warren has been particularly vocal about controlling and regulating the big tech companies. She ran for the US presidency and consequently has a published plan about what could be done to fix and regulate the big tech. Read all about it on this site.

## Washington Center for Equitable Growth
1156 15th Street NW, Suite 700
Washington, DC 20005
(202) 545-6002
email: njones@equitablegrowth.org
website: equitablegrowth.org/
The Washington Center for Equitable Growth is a non-profit research organization dedicated to promoting policy suggestions for strong, equitable economic growth. Read about the issue of big tech's four companies and economic results. Sign up for newsletter.

## World Economic Forum
350 Madison Avenue, 11th Floor
New York, NY 10017
(212) 703-2300
email: use links on contact page
website: www.weforum.org/

The World Economic Forum is an international organization dedicated to ensuring cooperation between public and private agencies around the globe. Watch videos, read articles, and sign up for their newsletter. Their website is full of information on issues important to people around the world.

# Bibliography

## Books

Alex Acks. *Key Labor Laws.* New York, NY: Cavendish Square, 2020.

Leighton Andrews. *Facebook, the Media and Democracy: Big Tech, Small State?* London,UK: Routledge, 2020.

Caleb Bissinger. *Tech Giants and Digital Domination.* New York, NY: Greenhaven Publishing, 2018.

Allum Bokhari. *#Deleted: Big Tech's Battle to Erase the Trump Movement and Steal the Election.* New York, NY: Center Street, 2020.

Floyd Brown and Todd Cefaratti. *Big Tech Tyrants: How Silicon Valley's Stealth Practices Addict Teens, Silence Speech, and Steal Your Privacy.* New York, NY: Bombardier Books, 2019.

Dedria Bryfonski. *The Global Impact of Social Media.* Detroit, MI: Greenhaven, 2012.

Scott Cleland. *Search & Destroy: Why You Can't Trust Google Inc.* St. Louis, MO: 2011.

Susan Crawford. *Fiber: The Coming Tech Revolution and Why America Might Miss It.* New Haven, CT: Yale University Press, 2018.

Alan M. Dershowitz. *The Case Against the New Censorship: Protecting Free Speech from Big Tech, Progressives, and Universities.* New York, NY: Hot Books, 2021.

Terri Dougherty. *Freedom of Expression and the Internet.* Detroit, MI: Lucent Books, 2010.

Roman Espejo. *Policing the Internet.* Detroit, MI: Greenhaven Press, 2012.

Rana Foroohar. *Don't Be Evil: How Big Tech Betrayed Its Founding Principles—and All of Us.* New York, NY: Currency, 2019.

Scott Galloway. *The Four: The Hidden DNA of Amazon, Apple, Facebook, and Google.* New York, NY: Portfolio/Penguin, 2018.

Josh Hawley. *The Tyranny of Big Tech.* Washington, DC: Regnery Publishing, 2021.

Mollie Hemingway. *Rigged: How the Media, Big Tech, and the Democrats Seized Our Elections.* Washington, DC: Regnery Publishing, 2021.

Raj Kumar. *The Business of Changing the World: How Billionaires, Tech Disruptors, and Social Entrepreneurs Are Transforming the Global Aid Industry.* Boston, MA: Beacon Press, 2019.

Anders Lisdorf. *Demystifying Smart Cities: Practical Perspectives On How Cities Can Leverage the Potential of New Technologies.* New York, NY: Apress, 2020.

Nicolas Petit. *Big Tech and the Digital Economy: The Moligopoly Scenario.* Oxford, UK: Oxford University Press, 2020.

Mike Rothschild. *The Storm is Upon Us: How QAnon Became a Movement, Cult, and Conspiracy Theory of Everything.* Brooklyn, NY: Melville House, 2021.

James P. Steyer. *Which Side of History?: How Technology Is Reshaping Democracy and Our Lives.* San Francisco, CA: Chronicle Prism, 2020.

Andrew Weiss. *The Dark Side of Our Digital World: And What You Can Do About It.* Lanham, MD: Rowman & Littlefield, 2020.

Alexis Wichowski. *The Information Trade: How Big Tech Conquers Countries, Challenges Our Rights, and Transforms Our World.* New York, NY: HarperCollins Publishers, 2020.

## Periodicals and Internet Sources

Paul M. Barrett, "Big Tech Doesn't Censor Conservatives: A Careful Review of Evidence Shows That's Fake News," *New York Daily News*, February 2, 2021. https://www.nydailynews.com/opinion/ny-oped-no-big-tech-doesnt-censor-conservatives-20210202-mwro7qspxrapjatqcevf6lrroa-story.html.

Shannon Bond, "Unwelcome on Facebook and Twitter, QAnon Followers Flock to Fringe Sites," NPR, January 31, 2021. https://www.npr.org/2021/01/31/962104747/unwelcome-on-facebook-twitter-qanon-followers-flock-to-fringe-sites.

Matthew Feeney, "Conservative Big Tech Campaign Based on Myths and Misunderstanding," CATO Institute, May 28, 2020. https://www.cato.org/commentary/conservative-big-tech-campaign-based-myths-misunderstanding.

Jamie Gangel, "Talk of Overturning the 2020 Election On New Social Media Platforms Used By QAnon Followers Sparks Fears of Further Violence," CNN, June 2, 2021. https://www.cnn.com/2021/06/02/politics/telegram-qanon-trump-supporters/index.html.

Evan Halper, "How Conservative Anger at Big Tech Pushed the GOP Into Bernie Sanders' Court," *Los Angeles Times*, May 6, 2021. https://www.latimes.com/politics/story/2021-05-06/how-big-tech-pushed-the-gop-into-the-corner-of-bernie-sanders.

Clara Hendrickson, "Big Tech Threats: Making Sense of the Backlash Against Online Platforms," Brookings, May 28, 2019. https://www.brookings.edu/research/big-tech-threats-making-sense-of-the-backlash-against-online-platforms/.

Mark Hosenball, "FBI Warns that QAnon Followers Could Engage in 'Real-World Violence'," Reuters, June 15, 2021. https://www.reuters.com/world/us/fbi-warns-that-qanon-followers-could-engage-real-world-violence-2021-06-14/.

Chase Johnson, "Big Tech Surveillance Could Damage Democracy," The Conversation, June 3, 2019. https://theconversation.com/big-tech-surveillance-could-damage-democracy-115684.

Klon Kitchen, "Big Tech's Big Problem: They Don't Understand the People," The Heritage Foundation," October 28, 2020. https://www.heritage.org/technology/commentary/big-techs-big-problem-they-dont-understand-the-people.

Sarah Kopit, "Why Big Tech and Conservatives Are Clashing on Free Speech," Bloomberg, January 11, 2021. https://www.bloomberg.com/news/articles/2021-01-12/why-big-tech-u-s-conservatives-battle-over-speech-quicktake.

Billy Perrigo, "Big Tech's Business Model Is a Threat to Democracy. Here's How to Build a Fairer Digital Future," *TIME*, January 22, 2021. https://time.com/5931597/internet-reform-democracy/.

Rachel Simmons, "How Social Media is a Toxic Mirror," *TIME*, August 19, 2016. https://time.com/4459153/social-media-body-image/.

Noah Smith, "Noah Smith: The Problem With Big Tech," *Pittsburgh Post-Gazette*, June 18, 2021. https://www.post-gazette.com/opinion/2020/08/04/Noah-Smith-The-problem-with-Big-Tech-Facebook-Google-technology/stories/202008040018.

Chris Talgo, "Big Tech's Assault on Free Speech," The Hill, August 4, 2020. https://thehill.com/opinion/technology/510367-big-techs-assault-on-free-speech.

Patrick Wintour, "US Seen as Bigger Threat to Democracy Than Russia or China, Global Poll Finds," *Guardian*, May 5, 2021. https://www.theguardian.com/world/2021/may/05/us-threat-democracy-russia-china-global-poll.

# Index